LOOKING ASTERN

By

Ed Ries

To my friend Hank
Enjoy a few storys from the past

Mike
12-20-12

Published by Monterey Publications
25572 Sarita Drive, Laguna Hills, California 92653

Cover: The author with nine albacore, taken with flylined anchovies on a South Coast Sportfishing magazine charter trip aboard Gary Black's CAT SPECIAL, 20 June 1985.

Monterey Publications
25572 Sarita Dr.
Laguna Hills, CA 92653

Ries, Edward M. 1919-
    Looking Astern

    1. Title 2. Fishing Barges 3. Fishing-California Ocean 4. -History
    5. -Tackle 6. -Techniques 7. -Sport 8. -Pier 9. -Commercial
    10. -Tuna 11. -boats 12. -Saltwater 13. Trolling

ISBN 978-0-9679247-2-4

Printed in the USA.

ACKNOWLEDGEMENTS

As before, my sincere thanks to all who have helped make this book possible, especially my publisher Steve Lawson and those who have kindly sent me historic items from their own collections: Richard Chikami, Bob Kocher, Jimmy Ziegler, Lynn Hollingsworth, and others. By sharing your stories and pictures you help us all revisit the past and share the wondrous experience of West Coast fishing as it was in the Golden Years. Special thanks are also due to the editors and publishers of *South Coast Sportfishing* and *Pacifc Coast Sportfishing* for giving continuous space to my columns and articles for 30 years.

Ed Ries
June, 2011

PHOTO CREDITS

The illustrations used in this book are from the author's collection assembled over many years. The majority are old copies of copies of copies and the original photographers' identities are lost in the mists of time. Many were received in the mail from kind readers of my columns and books, others are from multiple sources such as NOAA, California Dept. of Fish & Game, Long Beach Public Library, San Diego Maritime Museum, Portuguese Historical Society, San Pedro Bay Historical Society, and long-defunct newspapers and magazines. The personal collections of Lynn Hollingsworth, Richard Chikami, Jim Ziegler, Bob Kocher and Michael McCorkle have also provided items. My sincere thanks to all contributors for enabling readers to enjoy fascinating glimpses of the ocean fishing scene long past and current.

Ed Ries, the Ancient Mariner still fishes. The author bendo on a spotted bass in San Diego Bay.

Contents

Part I LOOKING ASTERN

Part II MIKE McCORKLE, THE ECLECTIC FISHERMAN

PART I

LOOKING ASTERN

281. THE LONGEST WHARF IN THE WORLD, AT SANTA MONICA

Santa Monica's famous Long Wharf furnished fabulous fishing, 1893-1920.

Popularity of pier fishing is evident in this photo of Newport Beach Pier.

Chapter 1

PEERLESS PIERS

Pier fishing was so popular a century ago that special trains for fishermen departed at 5 A.M. on weekends from the Los Angeles downtown terminal to Santa Monica Bay's Long Wharf and to Redondo. In the so-called Crescent Bay, there were piers every mile or so from the Long Wharf to Redondo including those at Santa Monica, Ocean Park, Venice, Del Rey, Hermosa, and Manhattan Beach. Redondo piers were renowned for frequent runs of yellowtail. Piers and wharves inside San Pedro Bay furnished great croaker fishing and Long Beach's Pine Avenue Pier was a base for some of the earliest charter and head boat fishing operations. Almost every California coastal town down to and including Imperial Beach had its fishing pier and they all provided excellent sport from time to time. Surf fishing from the beaches was also popular with those who had proper tackle.

Relatively few anglers had expensive rods and reels so most used handlines or jackpoles, which could be rented at the piers. For bait mussels and salted fish could hook many varieties and live bait could be "jerk-snagged" on "Japanese flies," the ancestor rig of the sabikis of today.

Halibut were prized for eating, but not considered a game fish. Bonito, mackerel and barracuda furnished summer excitement. Yellowtail were frequent biters also. All kinds of perch, often reported simply as "surf," croakers, sargo and butterfish were taken in huge quantities. The butterfish are known as pompano and news reports tell of anglers catching them two and three at a time and taking home 30 pounds or more of the tasty small critters.

Another very popular prey was queenfish, known then and as late as the 1960s as "herring." They were important enough to be included in the newspaper fishing reports and taken by a method known as "bobbing for herring." The large ones of 10 or more inches are also fair but bony eating and I remember spending a lot of time fishing for them as a youngster using fresh dead pinhead anchovies. Neither the official name nor the common name was really appropriate as there is nothing queenly about them, nor are they remotely related to true herring, which are closer to sardines.

A cousin was the kingfish, commonly called "tomcod," often so abundant they were considered a nuisance and scorned as worm-infested. Even so, large numbers were and are eaten. I caught them by the hundreds in my commercial set-lining days and they were always saleable, albeit for very low prices. So inappropriate is the name kingfish that the embarrassed Department of Fish & Game finally changed the official name to white croaker. Today the "royal" fishes are known as brown bait. They are not very strong or active swimmers, but halibut, kelp and sand bass love them and I have even hooked yellowtail with them.

Pompano, or butterfish (Peprilis sinillinus) is a tasty morsel once a favorite target of pier anglers.

The queenfish (Seriphus politus) was better known as herring and now as brown bait. Seldom seen in San Diego bait tanks.

Tomcod, kingfish or white croaker (Genyonemus lineatus) is the disreputable poor relation of the croaker family and gets no respect.

Santa Monica's Famous Long Wharf

In 1932, on one of my first ventures aboard a "live bait boat," I was introduced to a famous fishing hole. Aboard the Morris half-day boat FAITH, we were drifting about three miles north of the pier over a bottom studded with rubble and debris. Halibut were the target, but sand bass, sheephead, and sculpin were also caught. The spot was known as Long Wharf and was the location of one of the longest piers ever built. The bottom junk was left by sailors, laborers and fishermen during the 27-year life of the structure.

Known as Port Los Angeles, the pier was built in 1893 as a facility for berthing ocean-going cargo ships.

The wharf extended 4,720 feet, and 5,084 pilings and 4 million board feet of lumber were used in its construction. Included in its design was a fishing platform 12 feet wide and 600 feet long with a boat house and boarding ladder, 1,200 feet from shore. The dense stand of wooden pilings was a prime fish attractor.

After government engineers decided in 1897 on San Pedro for the official port, shipping activity gradually waned. In 1908 the wharf was leased to the Los Angles Pacific Railroad. The rail tracks were electrified, trolley wires strung, and daily trips for fishermen and sightseers were scheduled. It was an immensely popular attraction and fishermen could ride to the very end of the pier. There were several hundred poles for rent at R. A. Muller's Bait and Tackle shop.

All kinds of fish were caught and there were plenty of surface fighters such as yellowtail, barracuda and bonito available. Handlines and jackpoles were the primary tackle, along with rods fitted with crude sidewinder reels. Divers working the site find sidewinder remains to this day.

One of the main attractions was the availability of halibut, then, as now, a prized food fish. On August 17, 1917 a huge halibut measuring five feet, eight inches in length and four feet, two inches across the back, was caught from the wharf. The "barndoor" flattie weighed 62 plus pounds and reportedly took 40 minutes to land.

In 1920, due to the cost of needed repairs and upkeep, the pier was dismantled.

Coronado Pier

Few people today are aware that a fishing pier and breakwater for a boat basin once existed adjacent to the famous old Hotel del Coronado erected in 1888. Hotel guests and fishing addicts from San Diego made fabulous catches there, and their exploits were recorded in weekly newspaper articles published in Los Angeles and elsewhere.

Aerial view of Hotel del Coronado, boat basin and pier.

10

Charter sailboats and skiffs were available to explore the kelp bed that flourished a mile offshore. Quaint antique photos of the giant seabass, yellowtail and other gamefish taken nearby attest to the excellence of the fishing.

Fascinating accounts contain details and fish counts that boggle the mind. Many yellowtail were taken from the pier as well as from boats. Croakers, halibut, barracuda and bass were routinely numerous in the counts. Accurate identification of some species reported is questionable, as several common names then are no longer in use. For example, the hundreds of "trout" caught were obviously white seabass or shortfin corvina. Bonito were "Spanish mackerel." Kingfish hooked from the pier were possibly white croakers, known in my youth as tomcod, but that species is not as common in San Diego waters as it is farther north.

One reporter captured the essence of pier fishing's appeal when he opined, "Pier fishing is the fad nowadays among fishermen who have a thirst for the sea, but no sea legs. There they are on the sea and terra firma too. The sea surrounds them and the fish come right up to bite, while the pier is much more comfortable than a swaying boat."

I cannot resist the urge to share some of the news stories with readers who have an interest in our fishing history. Following are some slightly edited samples from the year 1898:

"In a two hour trip to Point Loma banks on Mrs. Greenwall's yacht guests caught 50 fish ranging in weight from 8 pound barracuda to 37-pound yellowtail. All around were seen smacks and sloops with fishermen hauling in the prey as fast as they could prepare the lines. All the boats returned early having as many fish as they could dispose of. On the pier 24 big yellowtail from 15 to 30 pounds were caught. Many Spanish mackerel were caught and hundreds more could be seen swimming about in the clear water. Three anglers went to the surf at dusk and caught 73 croakers in an hour and a quarter."

July 1, 1898: "Inspired by reports of a 50-pound sea trout captured near the Zuniga jetty, Messrs. Evans and Smith rented a skiff and encountered big yellow-

A slaughter of croakers was not unusual.

tail in the area. Evans boated one after taking a turn of his handline around an oar as the fish towed the skiff. Smith tied a line around his wrist and was yanked overboard and pulled away and under by a charging monster yellowtail. Evans took up the oars in pursuit and managed to cut the line from Smith's upraised wrist and drag his half-drowned companion into the boat. The yellowtail was estimated to be at least 30 pounds. After coughing up a gallon of sea water, Smith said he tied the line on his wrist by mistake and would make sure that it never happened again."

"The little sloops brought in a total catch as follows: 675 barracuda, 69 Spanish mackerel, 43 yellowtail, 60 halibut, 35 sea bass, total 875. This did not include Captain Jimmy Dunne's catch of 30 China croakers, one black bass, made just before breakfast just off the hotel, nor does it include fine quiet fishing off the pier where one man carried away 18 fine pompano besides a number of cheaper fish."

The Coronado pier and Hotel Del.

These formally clad anglers are fishing from a San Diego Bay wharf. Three are using handlines and three have cane jackpoles.

"When he discovered what he had, he played the big fish carefully and then walked it to the beach to be landed because it would be impossible to raise him to the gaff without parting the line. He gradually worked along the pier toward shore. Then, getting off the pier onto the beach, he waited for an extra big wave to come upon which to a land the fish. When it came he gave a steady pull which carried the salmon along on the crest of the wave to within 20 feet of shore. Then the young fellow waded in and grabbed the fish and wrestled with it till he hauled it in. The sight was witnessed by many people who came became greatly excited over the maneuvers of capture."

"Captain Dunne caught 40 small silver salmon in the morning. Total results for pier fishermen were 40 pompano, 230 kingfish, eight halibut, 53 silver salmon, 25 flounders, 90 croakers."

August 8, 1898: "Top trollers outside caught 250 barracuda, 60 halibut and 40 sea bass yesterday. Rock cod have been caught lately in good numbers. This is a very fine fish for eating, though the sport of catching it is not so great as with yellowtail or Spanish mackerel. Captain Dunne was out in a skiff last evening at dusk fishing just outside the surf in front of the hotel. He hauled in surf fish, croaker, corbina and perch galore, until he was tired. In all he caught 80 fish in an hour and a half."

"The total catch at the pier was about 250 and included pompano, corbina, perch, kingfish, mackerel, silver salmon, sand bass and lobsters. Sometimes there are entirely too many lobsters(!) Anglers hauling in their lines to fix the bait frequently pull up two or even more lobsters, impaled on the back or sides on the little hooks."

Sept. 13, 1898: "Anglers yesterday had excellent sport on the pier. One man went home on his wheel [bicycle] with a big yellowtail over his shoulder, almost as long as himself. The run of pompano, kingfish and croaker has been very good. The yellowtail caught at the pier did not exceed five, but they were all good sized, the largest weighing 28 pounds.

December 2, 1898: "A young man was fishing for yellowtail and Spanish mackerel and had a two-pound croaker on as bait. He was not looking for anything bigger than a 30-pound yellowtail, and was accordingly surprised when his frail line was snapped taught by a monster that began to circle the boat and puff like a locomotive."

"The fishermen hastily played out 500 or 600 feet of line up, but even this was insufficient and to save the line from being broken he and his companion got out the oars and rowed the boat after the big fish. Fortunately they prevented the breaking of the line. As gently as they could, they began to haul in, but the big fish resented this with a flip of his tail and a shake of his head like a vicious horse. After a struggle of an hour and twenty minutes the big fellow was tired out and drawn to the rail where he was dispatched with a marlinspike. Weighed at the warehouse he tipped the scales in a trifle over 350 pounds. It was the largest jewfish caught so far this season when he took the bait he was about two miles west of the hotel and when killed was a mile from that place."

"Total catch yesterday was 95 halibut, 15 Spanish mackerel, 25 rock cod, 40 lobster, total 276."

Redondo's three piers were excellent fishing platforms.

Redondo Piers

Among the most popular of the piers in the old days were those at Redondo, originally built to service ocean cargo ships. Proximity to a deep canyon on the sea bottom funneled pelagic fishes toward the shore and within reach of pier anglers. In June of 1907 the Los Angles & Redondo Railway scheduled Fishermen's Specials to leave the downtown terminal at 5 A.M. every Sunday and holiday.

Reports of takes as high as 100 "cornfed" mackerel for cane polers and handliners drew the crowds. At the time, fresh mackerel were held in higher esteem as food than they are today. To quote the unnamed reporter: "Many of these fish have been as much as a foot in length. The best bait for the mackerel is the mackerel steak, cut from the side of the first ones caught. There have been many good catches during the week with the Jap fly bait, the fish rising to it if it is sunk and jerked about a bit."

In October of 1907 the "greatest run of fish in the history of Redondo occurred when an immense school of yellowtail took possession of the waters around wharf No.1. The whole town turned out for the sport. "William Dolan brought in 17 big fellows. 'The scene was indescribable,'" he said, 'and I never saw such a sensational fishing day. The wharf was jammed with fishermen and it was impossible for this reason to use a rod and reel.' It appears that the yellowtail followed in a huge school of squid. 'The yellowtail were so thick that they actually turned the water brown. And that isn't a fish story, either,' declared Mr. Dolan."

On Sept. 23, 1908: "R. W. Deig caught the grand daddy of all yellowtails while fishing from Wharf No. 3. The fish weighed 50½ pounds and measured 54 inches in length. It is the largest yellowtail ever caught here and was brought to gaff with a 21-thread Cuttyhunk line after a royal battle lasting one hour and 55 minutes."

Fishing at Redondo was not always sensational, but the pompano, perch, croakers and halibut bit with a regularity that preserved its fishing reputation.

San Pedro & Long Beach Piers

Fishing in San Pedro Bay was excellent for croakers, queenfish, perch and lesser species in the early 1900s. A report in the *Los Angeles Herald* for 15 December 1905 tells us, "Fishing for yellowfin off the wharves is the best now it has been in the knowledge of the oldest inhabitant. In the last three days hundreds of the big fellows have been pulled out and there seems to be no let up in the run. Between 9 and 12 o'clock today 148 were taken out on the east side and something over 200 on the west side and not one of them weighed less than five pounds."

Winter fishing was good in January 1908 when "Good catches were made. Several spotfins averaging eight pounds or better were taken on light tackle and the man who was fortunate enough to get a strike from one of these big beauties was given all the fun he wanted in bringing it to gaff.

"The China croaker [sargo] was plentiful and of good size, fish running in weight from 1½ to 2½ pounds."

In August 1908 the channel was being deepened and those who took a small boat to the vicinity of the big dredger made good catches of croakers chummed by the clams and worms churned out by the digging.

The Long Beach Pier attracted huge crowds also and an item for 15 July 1908 declares that, "Bobbing for herring has paid big dividends for the capital and labor expended, and croakers are biting well. If you want a place to sit and fish off this pier you pretty nearly need to have a reservation."

This gent proudly displays his catch of 134 "cornfed" mackerel taken at San Pedro, 1915.

San Francisco enjoyed great pier fishing in November 1897 when a run of "grilse" (young salmon) headed for the Sacramento River. Fish weighed one half to six pounds.

13

Capt. Henry Schilling's auxiliary schooner SANTA BARBARA carried fishing parties from Long Beach in 1890s.

TOURIST returning from a trip. Four men, four women and a boy are on deck. Seating was in folding chairs. Gent in bow with the only visible rod and reel shows off with a giant bass.

Chapter 2
FISHING AFLOAT

Partyboat Beginnings

So abundant were all species of ocean fish along our coast a century ago that it is difficult to imagine. Huge catches were routinely made. Albacore were often found along the edges of the kelp beds and kelp bass, barracuda, yellowtail and albies could be taken on the same trip.

The first boats to venture out with paid passengers were propelled with sails or oars and did not travel far from their safe havens. After gasoline engines were developed larger boats were built and some filled dual purposes such as harbor ferries and freight haulers in addition to fishing. Apart from the 16-to-20 foot launches of the Avalon guides, which were built for use in calm waters in the lee of the island, the boats operating from the mainland were larger and often carried limited open-party trips.

Sportfishing from boats usually involved trolling with handlines or fishing with fresh dead, salted, or chunked bait. Yellowtail, albacore, barracuda and bonito were the most frequent trolling catch. Only a small fraction of anglers had rods and reels and few of the larger boats were suited for their use.

Pine Avenue Pier at Long Beach, opened in 1893,

became a center of boating activity. Fascinating reports from old newspaper clippings tell of the catches made. Boats mentioned are the SANTA BARBARA, EAGLE, CAMAGUIN, TWILIGHT, POINT LOMA and TOURIST, among others. San Pedro and other sites such as the Long Wharf, Venice Pier and Redondo Pier in Santa Monica Bay also had a few charter boats and rental skiffs.

Several of the early Long Beach headboats were former harbor ferries with canopies over the open decks. Not more than three or four lines at a time could be drug from the narrow hulls without tangles. Unsuited for the use of rods and reels, they carried handliners for bottom fishing and trolling.

TOURIST had a more modern appearance and configuration and more fishing room than canopied boats. This type hull was standard for fishboats for the next 25 years.

In an item dated October 3, 1909, Capt. Al Shook reports that for the previous five months his boat TOURIST made 114 trips carrying 894 passengers. Their catch: 4,123 bass, 320 barracuda, 309 halibut, 82 albacore, 39 yellowtail, 18 yellowfin (croakers), 6 sheephead, 2 trout (white seabass), 1 bonito and 2 jewfish (giant seabass), each and the boat obviously fished more at anchor than by trolling, thus saving expensive

View from towed skiff of handline trolling from San Diego boat GOLDEN WEST. A yellowtail is being boated.

gasoline and allowing all hands to fish at the same time. They had no small live bait such as anchovies or sardines, which only began to be carried in deck tanks on sportboats in the early 1920s. Again, it is old newspaper clippings that give us insight into fishing afloat as it was a century ago.

June 3, 1906: "Mr. and Mrs. Walter A. Stahlman, Charles Wonderly and Mrs. A. C. Ward chartered the launch TWILIGHT under the guidance of Captain Graves and had a delightful fishing trip off of Long Beach, bringing in a large catch of yellowtail and barracuda."

December 20, 1906: "Deep sea fishing boats which came in last night reported the best luck of the year. The EAGLE brought in 1,000 pounds of grouper, rock cod and bonito. The CLEMENTE 250 pounds; the CAMAGUIN 250 pounds; and the MAYETTA 250 pounds. After the passengers on the EAGLE had carried home big bundles of fish, Captain Paschall sold to a local market the remainder, weighing 550 pounds net."

November 6, 1907: "A monster jewfish [giant black seabass] was brought in last night by the CAMAGUIN, Captain H. H. Mason. It is estimated that the weight of the monster is nearly 600 pounds. The fish is seven feet long. It was caught by C. J. Richardson, an employee on the fishing boat."

December 28, 1907: "All Southern California records for jewfish catching have been surpassed by Clarence Owens of this city, who this morning caught his 24th monster of this variety since December 1. The jewfish have averaged about 300 pounds in weight. On several different days Owens has caught two jewfish. The fishing boat CAMAGUIN last night brought in 1,000 pounds of deep sea fish."

February 17, 1908: "The oldest resident cannot recall a time when a larger catch a fish was brought in on a single local boat than that which the CAMAGUIN carried last night when she tied up at the outer wharf after a day on the banks. The catch of weighed 2,762 pounds. The fishing party, besides Captain Mason, owner of the boat, included seven passengers.

April 8,1908: "E. E. Hall of San Pedro took two light tackle experts in the launch LUKE KELLY and made an excellent catch Tuesday. Running offshore from point Vincente eight barracuda, six bass, one whitefish and 22 albacore were caught within 6 hours. One of the party is a St. Louis merchant and he took a 28 pound albacore in 43 minutes. He was enthusiastic in his praise of channel fishing and said he would spend many more days at the sport before going back east."

September 13, 1908: "Hen Berry and his party of press boys spent several hours most pleasantly riding over the big blue waves, or words to that effect, about 16 miles out from San Pedro and the net results of the trip were 21 fine albacore, averaging 25 pounds each, and great sport.

"No less than 40 fish escaped from the hooks after being drawn up near the boat, which makes the history of the trip more worthy of consideration. The features of the trip were in Berry's hard luck in failing to get a bite until late in the afternoon and his remarkable luck afterward. After trying for two hours in the early morning and failing to get a strike he went to sleep. He awoke about 3 o'clock and carelessly threw in his line because the boys were kidding him as the only failure on the trip. Instantly it was snapped by an albacore and all was excitement. Then for the next half hour Hen dragged them in regularly, and every time he landed one he would yell out in derision at the small catches of the others. Hen got about seven of the 21. About eight anglers per trip averaged

Catch from PASTIME in 1900 included yellowtail, barracuda and bonito.

16

The launch LUKE KELLY with 18 large albacore and what appears to be a giant sunfish for two anglers, 1908. The boat looks not to be not over 24 feet in length and not well-suited for offshore work.

around five fish caught."

September 24, 1909: "G. L. Garnock, a rancher, yesterday caught the biggest yellowtail ever seen on Long Beach Pier. Garnock was fishing from the launch EAGLE. He had a strenuous battle or 23 minutes with the big fish, but finally landed it with the assistance of Captain Paschall. The fish weighed 46 pounds."

January 7, 1910: "Two six-foot blue sharks caught on one deep sea line of the fishing boat EAGLE afforded no little excitement last evening. During the fight the sharks succeeded in tangling the 20 lines on the boat so

the big fish were brought in together with difficulty."

October 10, 1909: "A 135-pound jewfish was caught with a rod and line yesterday afternoon by Guy Griffith and Robert Cox, fishing from a skiff some distance east of the pier. The fish fought the men for an hour, and Cox's right thumb was burned severely by the flying line when the fish ran out with 600 feet of the cord. The fish was brought to the pier."

November 8, 1909: "The perseverance of W. E. Gilman, a local musician, won him laurels today in a new fishing stunt, when a 10-foot shark pulled him overboard from his tiny powerboat AENID. Gilman was followed into the ocean by is engineer, Al Elmore, who grasped at the other man in an effort to save him from going over. Gilman retained his hold on his fishing rod and with

On 13 September, 1908, Hen Berry and pals got 21 albacore on the LUKE KELLY.

Handline trollers took 101 yellowtail and barracuda on the POINT LOMA in 1898.

Elmore's assistance climbed into the boat. He and Elmore then landed the fish; it probably weighed 80 pounds. The head was severed and brought to the pier"

November 15, 1909: "Mr. and Mrs. Ed Caley of Los Angeles and Binner Whitaker will fish for groupers at San Pedro Sunday going out in the MISCHIEF. This is a regular outing for this party, and last Sunday in the launch NELLY eight miles out they landed 2,400 pounds of groupers."

December 15, 1909: "An exciting time was that of two Long Beach fishermen, Clarence Owens and William Hayes, when they paid their usual daily visit to Owens' setline, some distance from the pier. Owens found that two jewfish were on his line and that others of the same species had made off with three of his hooks. He started in to bring one of the monsters to gaff, and a battle royal ensued. For over half an hour he fought the big fish, which whirled the boat round and round. When the fish was brought to gaff and subdued by a succession of blows rained upon its cranium the veteran fisherman was worn out."

A Monterey in Fish Harbor, 1929.

Classic Monterey Boats

In the years between the two world wars, hundreds of small one and two-man commercial boats plied California waters engaging in a variety of fisheries. The favorite vessel type for these activities was the Monterey clipper. Evolving from the design of late 19th century sailing feluccas of the Mediterranean the boats, in spite of their common name, were built mostly in the San Francisco Bay area and there were hundreds of them working from every port on the California Coast.

Montereys were usually built without formal plans by immigrant Italian boatwrights and ranged from 26 to 32 feet in length. For working fishboats their appearance is exceptionally pleasing. The sharp clipper bow flares widely to deflect spray and sweeps aft into a wide, full bodied hull sitting low in the water. The rounded canoe stern makes the boat safe and comfort-

able in a following sea and the low freeboard facilitates working lines, traps or nets. Many have a sharply crowned deck to shed sea water.

A cockpit or well in the stern allows for tiller steering and secure footing for handling gear. One or two-cylinder Hicks gasoline engines powered nearly all the boats when built, but most were modernized with more efficient engines in later years.

The design is so practical and well founded that a few survive to this day, long after small scale hook-and-line fishing has ended. Most of the surviving Monterey's are employed as salmon trollers, a task for which they are well suited. The hulls slip so easily and smoothly through the water that on my own boat I was able to lure albacore to strike on short handlines only 6 feet long.

At the peak of the local albacore fishery in the late 'teens and early '20s of the last century, they delivered 75% of the total albacore catch. When the longfins disappeared the boats were easily adapted to trolling for barracuda and setlining for bottomfish. Relatively few of the seaworthy classics survive, but they were once prominent features of the fishing scene in every port on the coast.

ALALUNGA.

Two Broad Beams

During the great postwar sportfishing boom two unusual vessels, ALALUNGA and BETTY LOU, came online. In compliance with the licensing regulations then in force, both were 65 feet in length. Most notable feature was their extremely wide beam of 22 feet, creating an ungainly, stubby-looking appearance. Hulls were of steel, superstructures of aluminum. Original power was twin 900 hp Sterling gasoline engines. Roomy lounges, galleys and bunk rooms were featured and the boats were popular with anglers favoring comfortable cruising and stable fishing platforms. Because of their inefficient hull design, fuel consumption was very high. On ALALUNGA's first and only trip to Catalina 500 gallons of high-test gas were consumed. As a result only local fishing was done until diesel engines were installed.

ALALUNGA was built for J. S. Barrett by the Central Boat Manufacturing Co. of Newport Beach. She made her first trip from the Port Orange landing on 12 August 1947. On that cruise to the 14 Mile Bank 22 passengers captured 33 albacore. A deckhand in her six-man crew was young veteran Bob Kocher, who had the foresight to gather and preserve an impressive collection of brochures, landing cards and news clips going back to the mid-1930s. Bob has very kindly shared many of his fishing mementos with us.

Later renamed INKSPOT, the boat was used to scoop squid commercially. Sold again, a new bow and stem added 15 feet to her length. She hauled sea urchins as a pickup boat and albacore and other fisheries were also tried. She may still be afloat wearing the name BOSS.

A sister to ALALUNGA was BETTY LOU, built for Louis Vance and home ported in San Diego. She too, was plagued by high operating costs. After a few seasons the hull was lengthened and for a short time she was at Paradise Cove. She later sank during attempts to use her as a freighter.

USS COURSER (AMc 32) in 1941.

Saga of NANCY ROSE

In 1940 naval planners, frantically preparing for apparently imminent war, were alarmed at the difficulties the British were having with mines in coastal waters. U.S. mine craft were obsolete holdovers from the First World War and few in number. For a quick fix, the Navy purchased over 40 large commercial fishing boats from 86 to 170 tons and refitted them for coastal minesweeping. Wooden-hulled West Coast purse seiners were deemed most suitable for the job, and their conversion was farmed out to the smaller boatyards. To man these vessels Naval Reserve divisions were mobilized and trained in 1940, and as the conversions were completed, the men were assigned

Postwar NANCY ROSE restored as a fishboat.

to crews. I was one of those men attached to USS COURSER (AMc 32), ex-NANCY ROSE.

NANCY ROSE was built at the Al Larson boatyard in 1938 for fisherman Tony Di Leva and named for his sister. She was stoutly constructed with sister keels for longitudinal strength. A 260 hp Superior diesel drove her, and a large bank of batteries provided electrical power. There were no electronic aids as we know them today.

The Navy made drastic changes to the former fish boat, including installation of a topside pilothouse and a huge generator in the fish hold to provide pulsing power for detonating magnetic mines. After some time spent in San Diego for shakedown and fitting out with naval stores, she returned to her homeport at the Section Base, San Pedro. Intensive training ensued with both magnetic and moored mine sweeping techniques. I was serving in her when war began but was transferred to an East Coast ship in January 1942 and lost track of the former purse seiner.

Her original owner had first refusal on her return after the war, but turned her down as he already had another boat. Wilbur Wood of Southern California Fish Co. bought her and leased her to three Americans of Japanese descent who had suffered forcible internment in relocation camps for the duration. George Fukuzaki was captain, Ben Fukuzaki was mastman and Minoru Chikami was chief engineer. These three and their crew of veterans were industrious and successful in the pursuit of tuna, sardines, and mackerel. Left aboard from her Navy days, NANCY ROSE had a Buda auxiliary and a Submarine Signal Fathometer, hard to get at the time and a definite advantage for her crew.

Young Richard Chikami, son of Minoru, began learning the ways of the sea and its fish on local trips at the

19

age of eight. He grew up to carry on the family fishing tradition and became a successful captain and chief engineer of modern tuna vessels. Now retired, he is also a diligent fishing historian and has very kindly shared much valuable information with me. That he and I trod the same decks on NANCY ROSE becoming acquainted over 50 years later due to our mutual interests, is to us an interesting coincidence.

In the late '50s the boat was sold to Louisiana owners after the fishing family obtained a newer vessel. She worked on in the Gulf of Mexico shrimp fishery and disappeared from the rolls in 1979.

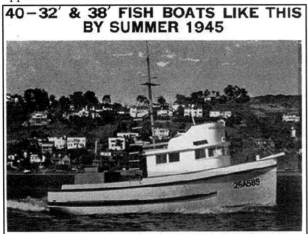

Famous Kettenburg Albacore Boats

After the government requisitioned around 50 large tuna clippers during World War II, many fishermen were unemployed. The authorities made allocations of wood and other materials necessary to construct a series of smaller fishing boats. Among the most brilliant designs were those of George Kettenburg, Jr., proprietor of the Kettenburg Boat Works on San Diego's Point Loma.

From 1944 to 1949, the yard's skillful craftsmen, using only the finest materials available, turned out 80 boats. Most were rigged with bait tanks, but some were strictly trollers. The boats could be fished by as few as two hands or as many as four. They proved to be ideal for chasing the albacore that had again found their way to Mexican and California waters.

Known as K-38s, the compact craft were excellent sea boats and very successful and popular. For example, the four White brothers migrated from the Middle West to make small fortunes in K-38s. Within a few years each had his own boat: Charlie's KITTY LEE, Chester's DOLCHESTER, Hubert's MARY B., and Wendell's QUIZ KID.

The round-bottomed vessels were 38 feet long with a 12-foot beam and were capable of carrying up to 10 tons of tuna in a refrigerated ice hold. Their 600-mile range

was often extended with extra fuel carried in 55-gallon drums on deck. Fitted with a gasoline engine and fully rigged, ready to fish, the cost was about $13,000, or $16,000 with diesel power. At the time, a decent new home could be bought for those sums.

My own cruises in Martin Stuart's K-38 DANNY BOY, in 1949 and 1955, provide valuable and cherished memories--the first for a catch of three-pole tuna and the second for some exciting "merry-go-round" stops when the fish were flying aboard "like silver rain." As a testimony to the excellence of their design and construction, about six K-38s were still fishing in the year 2000 and several have been converted to yachts.

CALIFORNIA MAID was a typical K-38.

Warship to Fishing Barge

The end of World War II left the Navy with hundreds of surplus vessels, mostly amphibious landing craft built as one-way transports for the invasion of Europe and the island-hopping campaigns in the Pacific. A great many of the famous Jimmy (GM) diesel engines and smaller boats were sold to fishermen at bargain prices. Plywood-hulled LCVPs and LCPs were converted to commercial trollers and pleasure boats. A 119-foot LCT (Landing Craft, Tank) was renamed IWO JIMA and used as a bait receiver and barge at Newport and Long Beach. At least one antisubmarine patrol craft, the BUCCANEER, was converted to a fishing barge that worked at Paradise Cove and Redondo.

Several LCI (Landing Craft, Infantry) were stripped down and used as barges, notably the ELSIE I and ELSIE II at Huntington Beach, ACE I at Dana Point, the DIXIE at Capistrano, and the MANANA and TRADEWINDS at Redondo. LCIs were 158-foot steel ships with 23-foot beam providing ample room for anglers. Somewhat larger were the LSMs (Landing Ship, Medium) which were reborn as the fishing barges C-COASTER and

BONNIE K, both at Redondo. The ELSIEs were short-lived, the number I sinking in 1951 and number II stranding in 1956. ACE I went ashore in 1948 and BONNIE K and DIXIE in the storm of 29 April 1951.

Except for a lone survivor at Redondo, barge fishing was finished by the mid-70s and all the wartime veterans had vanished, wrecked or scrapped. Of 912 LCIs of her class built for the war, only one survives today, the LCI 1091, a museum relic at Eureka, California. Instead of serving as a sportfishing barge after her Navy career, she was employed for 28 years as a floating fish cannery in Alaska and thus endured until acquired for her present service as a memorial vessel.

Barge DIXIE, a wartime LCI, wrecked in 1951.

A wartime LCI (Landing Craft, infantry) underway.

USS LSM 4 in her warpaint.

DIXIE stranded.

C-COASTER was a former LSM.

BUCCANEER was once a wooden-hulled subchaser.

Bait barge IWO JIMA was an ex-LCT.

Barge CALIFORNIA, another leftover from WWII.

MANANA at Redondo.

Hans Carstensen's MAY BELL was one of the first commercial boats converted to live bait sport fishing. A couple of planks have been installed for passenger seating and are supported on their after ends atop the curve of the caprail. No structure for a "head" is visible. This dandy catch of large yellowtail was probably taken mostly with handlines as only one rod and reel is seen. Note the cane jackpoles atop the pilot house. They were very efficient for hoisting the smaller surface fish such as barracuda, bonito, mackerel and kelp bass.

The Live Bait Boats

A news item dated October 11, 1913 tells of a remarkable catch of yellowfin tuna five miles off Venice Beach from the charter launch ORIENT, Captain Childs. The six anglers aboard "began trolling with artificial minnows. When they had reached a spot where the ocean seemed alive with tuna, a party of Japanese fishermen in the launch KATO, which was filled to capacity with tuna, conferred a bucket of live bait on the newcomers. The ORIENT party thereafter stayed in one spot and cast with live bait." They boated 37 tuna from 30 to 48 pounds, some on light three-six tackle. After such an experience, there is little doubt that shrewd sportfishing captains would get the message and invest in a net to catch live bait and tank to hold it.

Catching and keeping alive large quantities of small fish in easily accessible deck tanks fitted on mobile passenger-carrying vessels is the basis for the deep-sea fishing business we know today. California has the most modern, well-equipped sportfishing fleet in the world, capable of carrying anglers in safety and comfort on thousand-mile voyages to distant and exotic fishing sites. There are no other vessels anywhere in the world quite like them. Have you ever wondered how this live bait style of fishing began and developed to its present extraordinary status?

Trolling was the usual method of taking game fish at the turn of the last century, and small sailboats were often employed, providing there was sufficient breeze to move them. A wake undisturbed by engine noise or shaft bearing thump was well suited to trolling. Primitive gasoline engines were coming into general use, but were clumsy and low powered for their weight and dangerously prone to cause bilge fires. A limited number of small boats operated on a charter basis with no organized daily schedule and few could carry more than six passengers. Most fishing was done with handlines and salted bait was used on the anchor or drifting. Sardines, smelt, queenfish and sometimes anchovies were caught with small beach seines handled by two or three men and the amounts taken were minor. It was usually salted down in wooden tubs, but sometimes used as "fresh dead." Mackerel and bonito flesh, salted or chunked, was also used.

It had long been recognized that live bait was the fastest way to generate a strike from hungry fish. Fishing from the many piers that then lined the coast was extremely popular and bait fish were sometimes captured in large hoop nets suspended from cranes. Snag lines with leaders of silkworm gut armed with 10 or more small, shiny hooks, or what Charles F. Holder described as "Japanese flies," were used to snare live sardines, smelt and queenfish. Similar rigs in use today are called "sabikis." A minnow could be caught and immediately transferred to a hook as bait, but no suitable method had yet been devised for containing or keeping large quantities alive for more than a short time. On piers bait buckets pierced with small holes around the

Earliest type of live bait boat used for albacore fishing, c.1912. One at right has a minimal pilot house

top half could keep alive a few small fish when lowered into the sea on a rope.

Albacore, the long-finned tuna, were responsible for the introduction of live bait fishing on a large scale. Immigrant Japanese commercial fishermen pioneered the method, known to them for centuries, to increase their take of albacore when large quantities of the fish first became desirable for canning.

At the turn of the 20th century, albacore were incredibly abundant close inshore to the Southern California coast. Pollution and heavy traffic had not yet affected their habitat. So common they were called "pigs" and held in the same low esteem as mackerel are today, they were regarded as a nuisance by sports and commercials alike. Charles F. Holder, the founder of the Avalon Tuna Club, wrote in 1909 that the chief fishing area for albacore was two miles directly off Avalon. Once there it was not necessary to troll. The launch was allowed to drift and the boatman chummed with dead sardines or chunks. The albacore would soon appear as a ravenous horde, taking everything that was tossed over.

He wrote: "To test their tameness, impale a sardine on your gaff and lower it down. In a moment a thirty-pounder has seized it and you have gaffed him and lifted him in. But I advise you not to tell the story, as no one will believe it, though it is one of the easiest things to accomplish when these fishes are biting in their normal fashion."

After A. P. Halfhill canned the first batch of albacore tuna in 1906, the demand for "chicken of the sea" grew rapidly and within a short time the San Pedro and San Diego commercial boats were all in the hunt for longfins. The once-despised "pigs" were suddenly a valuable catch.

The standard commercial boats that first set out to harvest the albacore were small, 30 to 36 feet in length, round-bottomed with a horseshoe stern and a straight stem. Gasoline engines from eight to 15 hp were the norm. A low trunk cabin forward covered the engine and a couple of bunks. There was no pilot house. A folding mast was usual forward of the trunk. Aft there was a hatch covering a rather shallow hold and the after deck was clear for handling gear. One to three men usually made up the crew.

A few records from that time tell of typical trips from San Pedro. Catching sufficient small fish for bait was often difficult. The boats would leave the harbor as early as midnight and begin a search for bait at a chosen site. There was competition and crowding at areas near the harbor. Some boats chugged all the way to Catalina Island, anchoring off the Isthmus. A small skiff was put over and the bait net loaded and carried to the shore. There a set was made with the skiff and both wings of the small net hauled onto the beach. The captured minnows were salted into tubs and men and gear returned aboard the anchored boat. Cruising back towards the mainland, a couple of lures, usually homemade, were trolled. If the bait fish were large or few in number, they were cut into chunks. When a jig strike occurred, the boat stopped and albacore were chummed with the chunks and caught with baited handlines. If the tuna were large, over 20 pounds, they would be head gaffed, the smaller fish simply flung aboard. After each stop when fishing ceased the arduous work of beheading and gutting each albacore immediately commenced. During the first years of operation the canneries would not accept round fish and the catch had to be delivered to the cannery by two p.m. As more boats entered the fishery they were limited to a catch of a ton a day.

The first tanks for holding live bait were squat boxes little more than knee-high from the deck. Fresh seawater was bailed in with buckets dipped over the side on a rope. This wasn't as difficult as it sounds, as the boats had a low freeboard and were not very fast underway. When bait died, it was used to chum jigs or on handlines.

Using a blanket net to catch bait fish.

OWL was typical albacore chaser still in commercial mode when she began sportfishing c.1923. Note bait net on stern and giant bass being boated.

Top hamper has been removed on OWL in 1926 and bench seats have been installed, but no lifelines. Jackpoles are provided for customers. OWL had a long career under several owners.

Every boat soon carried its own "blanket net," for catching bait. The small mesh web was stretched between two poles, one at the bow and the other at the stern. A rope attached to the leadline pulled it up amidships to entrap the bait. Small fish were attracted, mostly at night, with lanterns and chum of meal or ground fish. Only small amounts of bait were caught with the blankets, but it enabled the successful use of lift poles. Japanese fishermen from San Pedro began using bamboo poles with the live bait and the method soon became standard on the larger boats. Special tuna hooks and lures made in Japan were ingeniously fashioned to be very sharp for easy penetration and strong enough to lift heavy fish. The feathered lure was so designed and weighted that when the line was slacked the hook fell free. Yankee fishermen called them "squids" or "strikers."

To excite the albacore a sort of bamboo cup was attached to a short limber pole and used to splash water around the baited hooks of the pole fishermen.

About 1912 the Mediterranean lampara roundhaul net was introduced and it proved so successful for catching bait that the design remained in use until the present time. The nets were pulled by a crew of four to six fishermen and with them huge amounts of live bait fish could be captured, often enough to supply more than one boat for a day of fishing.

Until recent times lampara bait nets supplied commercial and sportfishing boats alike. Now giant purse nets retrieved with huge power-driven reels on specially built boats furnish bait for whole fleets of sportfishers.

Tank design was improved to handle larger amounts of live bait. Engine-driven pumps for bait water were adopted and tank size grew to four or more feet in height. Fresh seawater was additionally aerated as it flowed through a shallow compartment atop the tank to fall like rain through numerous small holes. This design endured on many sport and commercial boats until World War II. Vast improvements in methods of handling live bait were discovered and tested in the big long-range tuna clippers during the expansion of that fleet after 1926. Catching and keeping alive huge amounts of live bait was vital to tuna fishing before synthetic web purse seines replaced pole fishing.

By 1914 Japanese fishermen were building larger and faster boats. A small pilot house was added amidships and bigger bait tanks were installed. Engine power was increased to 40 hp, or more. The larger vessels were able to more easily employ the effective lampara nets for catching bait. With increased efficiency the fishermen prospered and a large number of boats 40 to 65 feet in length entered the fishery. A sort of standard design was adopted with a mast and boom mounted behind the midship pilot house. Hulls of Japanese-owned boats were usually painted white with black trim. Bait tanks and inboard bulwarks were painted "tuna red." Italians preferred a royal blue trim and other ethnic groups adopted gray, green and brown. The vessel type was known generically as "albacore chasers." In the off-season for albacore, the boats supplied the canneries with sardines and mackerel.

The albacore bonanza also lured many salmon trolling boats from the North Coast. These were mostly of the type known as "Montereys," developed by Italian boatwrights. Hundreds of the seaworthy clipper-bowed, double ended classics were to be found in every California fishing port between the world wars. New trolling lures were imported to replace the metal salmon spoons. Bone and feathered jigs from Japan, cedar jigs and bluefish lures from the East Coast were all tried with varying success. The fish were pulled by hand from boats moving at six or seven knots. By 1926 an astonishing 75 percent of the total commercial albacore catch was made by trollers.

Until about 1920 most sportfishing boats trolled or used salted bait. When albacore became desirable the larger salt bait boats at Long Beach mounted outrigger poles dragging six lines to a side. Passengers took turns hauling in the catch.

After years of intense research, who first had the idea of using live bait on a regular basis on a scheduled open party sportfishing boat, remains unknown. It appears that almost overnight operators at several South Coast locations switched to using live bait. Best guess is it began between 1921 and 1923. It seems odd to me that the California Fish & Game mavins did not note it or publish information on the use of live bait on sportfishing boats.

Captain Thornton J. Morris was one of the first, converting his salt bait boats at Santa Monica to live bait in the early '20s. The result was spectacular catches of all species of desirable fish and by 1923 use of live bait on sportfishing boats was well established. Soon every pier and landing from Santa Barbara to the Mexican border offered live bait fishing on mobile party boats and anchored barges. "Live bait boats" became the generic term in general use by news reporters and fishermen alike to describe the popular new vessel mode. The phrase remained current through the 1930s.

Still, it was several years before the complete transition took place. Only the larger boats with open decks could be readily adapted. Many of the smaller trolling boats clung to their method and fishing reports until the late '20s described catches by both trollers and live bait boats. Nearly all were converted albacore chasers, especially in the early years. Safety regulations for small craft were vague and incomplete and creature comforts were often extremely rudimentary in the early conversions. A bench was provided for seating and a bucket and a few lifejackets tossed into the crew bunks in the forward hold were all that was necessary to fit a boat for carrying a load of eager anglers. Insurance provisions later required addition of a pipe and chain lifeline, a phone booth-sized "head" and a box atop the pilot house for cork lifejackets, A few other vessel types, such as the motor yacht KIAORA and ex-channel ferry MUSIC were also adapted. During her long life, the latter was first a salt bait boat, then a troller and finally a live bait boat. In 1934 SEA ANGLER the first sizeable built-for-the-purpose sportfisher, was launched in San Diego.

At first each boat had its own bait net and before proceeding to the fishing banks passengers frequently assisted in hauling the net. Where several party boats operated from one location, one catcher boat usually contracted to furnish bait for all.

After World War II there were a few old ex-commercial craft still operating, but these were soon replaced. Many surplus former naval vessels and newly constructed keel-up boats entered the booming sportfishing business. In a few short years the sportfishing fleet developed into the magnificent flotilla it is today.

Much near-shore fishing was done in skiffs, 1905.

Fishboat Evolution

The earliest California fishing boats to venture onto the seas were small and powered by oars or sails. Immigrant Italian fishermen in the San Francisco area built and sailed the lateen-rigged felucca, a design common in the Mediterranean Sea. The boats were seaworthy double-enders steered with a tiller. In other coastal areas the majority of sailboats were sloop-rigged "smacks." Those methods of propulsion endured until primitive gasoline engines were introduced in the late 1890s. A low trunk cabin was built to cover the engine and a couple of bunks, but steering was still by tiller in the stern. For fifty years the only aids to navigation were a simple box compass and a timepiece. Kerosene lamps were used for running lights.

As population and demand for edible fish grew, so did the numbers and dimensions of the boats. The shift to gasoline engines progressed rapidly, but for some years they were not fully trusted and with good reason. Most fishermen were unfamiliar with them and baffled by the mechanics. Gasoline was a dangerous fluid that required careful handling and storage. Bilge fires and explosions were not uncommon.

Attempts were made to motorize the felucca hulls with a propeller shaft through the side curve of the stern. The vibration and stress proved too much for light sailboats and around 1904 the first stoutly built "Monterey" type boats were launched in San Francisco Bay. The early boats had straight stems at the bow. The flared bow with the "chicken beak" and curved stem came in about 1910. That ultimate design was so practical and popular with independent-minded solo fishermen that hundreds were built over a long span of years. Montereys are the ideal vessel for trolling or other hook and line fishing by one or two men and they could be found in every port on the

San Pedro commercial boats c.1913. Only a couple have pilot houses. Tall masts forward are for sails in case of engine trouble. These boats have straight stems and horseshoe sterns wide enough to handle the covered nets.

coast. A few of those classics survive to this day.

Room for handling and stacking nets or mounting a live bait tank was obtained with a rounded or fantail-sterned boat of somewhat larger size and wider beam. A sort of basic fishboat became standard for lampara net and live bait fishing. The type were known as "albacore chasers" during the heyday of the local fishery for that species. The lampara albacore boats were from 36 to 50 feet in length with an enclosed pilot house amidships, a forward bunk room and a mast. They usually carried a crew of four to six fishermen.

As larger and more seaworthy hulls were built and more powerful engines installed, there were still concessions to the unreliability of the gasoline motors. Up until the early 1920s most vessels were equipped with a mast stepped near the bow so that a sail could be rigged in case of engine failure. A tall mast increased the tendency of the round-bottom hulls to roll in choppy seas. When more confidence was gained in the new engines the mast was usually hinged about four to six feet off the deck so that it could be lowered horizontally to rest on top of the midship pilot house. Fishermen used it as a rack for drying nets, ropes or clothing. Engines became more powerful and reliable and were fitted into bigger boats. With more room a small pilot house for the helmsman was built amidships. Larger nets were shipped and larger crews were needed to handle them. Sardines, mackerel and tuna were taken by the ton and it became desirable to have mechanical aid in loading and unloading the catch. Masts in newer boats were stepped amidships, immediately aft of the pilot house. The mast cold be braced with permanent shrouds and fitted with a boom carrying blocks and tackle for hoisting and moving heavy weights. This layout became prototype for the "tuna clippers," big boats built to cruise distant waters in the hunt for year-around sources of tuna. Steering and engine controls atop the pilot house were also installed on the larger boats to aid in visual fish spotting In the early 1920s when sport fishing entrepreneurs finally wised up to the advantages of fishing with live bait, it was simple and logical to buy a lampara albacore boat, sometimes including the bait net, and begin hauling loads of anglers. Few changes or modifications were needed. A couple of wooden planks were fitted along the after caprails for seating and a bucket and a few cork life jackets tossed into the forward bunk room. Suitable rods and reels for ocean fishing were still rare so most of the early "live bait boats" carried bundles of long bamboo poles for use by passengers. A lot of handline fishing was also done.

A great many of the early sportboats were thus converted and only a very few built-for-the-purpose boats were constructed before World War II. I know of only four, all in San Diego. They were Oakley Hall's SEA ANGLER and STAR ANGLER and Frank Kiessig's SPORTFISHER II and SPORTFISHER III.

A felucca under sail in San Francisco Bay.

Sloops like this were good trollers in a breeze.

All the prewar head boats I remember operating from Santa Monica Bay piers were converted commercial craft. A few others running from San Pedro and Long Beach were converted from other hulls, but all were originally some type of workboat, except one. She was the motor yacht KIAORA, rumored to be a onetime rum-runner in Prohibition days. She underwent several alterations during a long career that lasted into the post-war years. There were possibly one or two others, perhaps Dick Crank's RETREAT being one, and there were several small motor yachts doing charters.

When war began, all landings were closed and the boats were laid up, or commandeered for use as patrol, fire-fighting, diver service, etc. Some again engaged in commercial fishing when things settled down and a few even resumed sport fishing after the hostilities.

A huge surge of boat building began immediately after the war to satisfy the pent-up demand for recreation. Many veterans had dreams of owning a fishing boat and their savings were invested in new construc-

tion or acquisition and conversion of one of the hundreds of surplus hulls sold off by the government for a fraction of original cost.

New marine plywood had demonstrated its potential in the famous PT boats during the war. Plywood Naval landing craft such a LCVPs and LCPLs complete with diesel engines were popular for conversion work. The bow ramp was removed from an LCVP and the keel extended for a few feet. A vertical stem piece was added to which bent plywood pieces were fitted to form a pointed bow. None of these conversions had a long life as most of the makeshift bow sections eventually worked loose in rough seas. However, plywood new construction from the keel up was quite successful and some fairly large sport and commercial fishing vessels were launched or converted from aircraft rescue boats or fast bombing target vessels.

Two to five HP one-cylinder marine gasoline engines powered nearly 100 percent of early Monterey boats.

San Francisco rock cod boats with canoe sterns were the direct ancestors of the Montereys.

Conventional construction of wooden planked hulls also kept boatyards busy and a few steel and aluminum hulls were also tried. The old narrow, round bottom, horseshoe stern commercial conversion sportboats were a thing of the past. Most of the new sportfishers were designed with a hard chine, transom stern configuration that remains the current fashion. Many creature comforts for passengers are incorporated in modern boats and the long range vessels that spend continuous days at sea are the last word in safety equipment and electronic aids to navigation. Commercial fishing boats also have modern improvements necessary to keep abreast of ever-increasing competition for the sea's bounty. Modern tuna purse seiners, now mostly under foreign flags, are approaching the size of cruise liners and are capable of wrapping a hundred tons of fish in one set of their nets. Not a good development for a dwindling resource.

The following illustrations depict stages in the evolution of commercial and sport fishing boat design in California.

EAGLE was a headboat at Long Beach in 1905. The canopy made even handline fishing awkward.

A transitional canoe stern hull with a bait tank, a somewhat unusual arrangement for this design.

Launch EMILINE in San Pedro channel in 1909. Caption says she is "equipped with plenty of trolling tackle. Specializes in fishing parties, outings, etc."

In the late 1890s, small vessels used by charter boatmen at Catalina Island were okay in calm waters of the lee. Primitive engines were fueled by naptha or "gasolene vapor."

An older lampara boat waits to unload sardines along-side a modernized model with pilot house over engine.

Classic 26-foot Monterey, new in 1930, was typical of the hundreds of her type. She also has a folding mast.

A small pilot house and a folding mast forward were the next improvements for fantail stern lampara boats. A bait tank was added for albacore fishing, c.1916.

MOONLIGHT shows off catch of barracuda. She still has her forward step-hinge for a folding mast, c.1930.

Double bait tanks are a load for this commercial boat.

W.K. shows her obvious origin as a commercial lampara-albacore boat. At Santa Monica, prewar.

Modern steel tuna seiner BOLD ADVENTURESS.

Left: In 1925, new tuna boat ABRAHAM LINCOLN was an enlarged version of standard albacore chasers.

A century ago the abundant giant bass were really giants: 268, 109, 253, 251, and 326 pounds.

J. A. Coxe with tuna of 104, 156, 104, 114, 103 pounds. Guide is George Farnsworth.

Chapter 3
FABULOUS FISHES

Horse Mackerel

At Catalina, on June 1, 1898, Charles Frederick Holder took a bluefin tuna that weighed 183 pounds, an event that marked the beginning of sportfishing as we know it today. It was the first catch of a tuna over 100 pounds on rod and reel and the resulting publicity captured the attention of anglers worldwide. Holder's extensive writings about his fishing experiences lured wealthy anglers to the island from far and wide. As the bluefin frequently cleared the water in pursuit of flying fish, Holder called them "leaping tuna." Their Atlantic cousins were known as "horse mackerel."

Holder's tackle for the memorable catch consisted of an 8.5-foot, 40-ounce rod of greenheart wood and a Vom Hofe reel spooled with 200 yards of 21-thread "Cuttyhunk" linen line. The leader was eight feet of single-strand wire armed with a 7/0 hook. Bait was a 12-inch flying fish trolled about 60 feet back.

The reel had no brake other than a clicker and a leather thumb pad hinged to a crossbar. Drag was applied almost entirely by the right thumb. Some additional pressure was attained by squeezing the line against the rod's foregrip with the left hand. There was no freespool and outgoing line spun the handle backward with the viciousness of a buzzsaw. "Knuckle buster" was the kindest term coined for the dragless reel.

The boat was a tiny 16-20 foot launch with a backless bench seat for the fisherman. No rod harnesses were available and small leather socket belts provided only minimal protection for the angler's groin. It took Holder nearly four hours to conquer his big tuna and he wrote that it towed his launch for 10 miles. He was near collapse when the fish was finally brought to gaff and his exhaustion was such that he feared a heart attack. His arms were numb and all feeling had left his thumb.

Such fishing was no pastime for wimps. It took courage to tangle with a big tuna on the primitive tackle. It could be traumatic and one angler dislocated an arm while another "dropped senseless" as his 180-punder was gaffed after a five-hour battle.

Large bluefin were seldom caught in local waters after the 1930s. Small school tuna were taken at the Coronado Islands and Catalina, sometimes along the mainland coast and often with albacore schools. A few giants are occasionally found at Guadalupe Island, and fairly large fish are caught now and then, but these days if an angler wants to pit his strength and skill against really big tuna he must try for the cow yellowfin targeted by the long-range sport fleet.

Over 100 years ago Holder wrote of Catalina bluefin: "For hard fighting and persistence, force and strength, I award the palm to the tuna." I would agree 100 percent.

31

Bygone Bluefin

The last of the original runs of large bluefin tuna that motivated founders of the famous Tuna Club of Avalon occurred in 1931. Since that time large tuna in local waters have been exceedingly scarce, but smaller "school tuna" were often available. In the 1930s they were found at Catalina and the Coronado Islands and occasionally at the Horseshoe Kelp. Recently, these have also become scarce, bluefin appearing only intermittently with albacore and at the Cortes Bank. I have taken them near San Diego at the Coronado Islands, the Rockpile below the islands, at La Jolla and once at the Hill Street spot off Point Loma. There was a decent run at the Coronados in 1972 and I caught my last one in 1990 on a paddy-hopping trip for yellowtail. It was a dandy fish of over 30 pounds. Numerous yellowfins came my way since then, but no more bluefins. Physical infirmity now keeps me from offshore trips.

My first bluefin was taken from the San Pedro sportfisher SUNSHINE II at Catalina in 1937. Tuna were boiling all around the boat, but they were hook-shy in the gin-clear water. Only large "bohunk" sardines could be easily cast with reels fitted with heavy metal spools and sticky linen lines. An active, strongly swimming bait almost guaranteed a strike. By waiting patiently I was lucky enough to be twice awarded a sizeable sardine found by the chummer in the mix of pinhead anchovies crowding the bait tank. I caught a tuna with each of them.

A pinhead bait was too feeble to move the weight of a wire leader and linen line and too light to cast with the tackle then available. To overcome this frustrating disadvantage, several canny anglers spooled freshwater baitcast reels with braided silk line and fined down their leaders to a hair-thin number two wire and tiny number eight hook. Occasionally they would hook up a tuna, but it was extremely difficult to control a wild fish on a crowded party boat and the tuna usually escaped.

Other aids for casting small baits were a hollow clear plastic capsule about four inches long, partially filled with water, that had a hole in the center axis through which the line was passed and then attached to the leader. Red rubber balls about 2.5 inches in diameter with a center hole also provided enough casting weight to be tossed out 20 feet or so from the boat.

Certain old-time sportboat skippers were famous for their skill at coaxing spooky bluefin tuna to bite. Among them were Billy Rice, Dick Crank and the late Eddie McEwan, sometimes know as "Captain Bluefin" for his uncanny ability to find and catch the most elusive of Pacific tunas.

Edward Llewellyn caught the first marlin in 1903.

Catalina Billfishing in the Old Days

A century ago, when big-game fishing was in its infancy, the main focus of anglers at Santa Catalina Island was on large bluefin tuna. The famous Tuna Club of Avalon, founded in 1898 by Charles Frederick Holder and his fishing cronies, had no prizes or rewards for the capture of billfish.

Finally, in 1909, as billfish catches increased in number, their importance was recognized with appropriate prizes. Holder, ironically, in spite of an expressed desire to do so, never succeeded in catching either a marlin or a broadbill.

In his books, Holder usually describes both marlin and broadbill as "swordfish" and the reader at times has difficulty determining the species to which he is referring. He sometimes alludes to striped marlin as a "California spearfish" or as "Japanese swordfish."

Records show that the first marlin "swordfish" to be taken off Catalina on a rod and reel was landed in 1903 by E. B. Llewellyn. The lucky fisherman declared in an interview with Holder that "the fish made a fine fight and established its reputation as a thoroughly game fish. It fought hard. Its movements were exceedingly

C. G. Conn's 336-pound marlin was a record.

were acting in a blind panic and without intention. It is also possible that the tackle in use at the time was considered to be inadequate for fighting swordfish, but any gear that could stand up to a battle with giant tuna could certainly whip a marlin.

The usual heavy outfit for big game was a rod of greenheart, hickory or other wood, around seven feet in length. The ferrules that joined the butt and tip were often too weak and bent or broke under heavy strain. Mounted on the rod was a straight-handled knuckle buster reel with a leather thumb drag and a twisted linen line of 48-pound dry breaking strength. The reels frequently seized up tight after a short fight. Leaders were of single strand bronze or steel piano wire, vulnerable to kinking. Many fishing hands were mutilated by backward-spinning reel handles, whirling like airplane propellers as powerful fish raced away on desperate runs.

Ralph Bandini, a Catalina fishing pioneer, wrote that one corner of the porch at the old Metropole Hotel was dubbed "Tuna Hospital" when angry, injured anglers with bandaged hands and sprained shoulders gathered to nurse their wounds and sore egos as they griped about their bad luck.

A main drawback in billfishing would be the rapid switching in a marlin's fighting tactics, different than a tuna's and exceedingly hard to control with only 200 yards of line.

Searching for a better way to battle fish, dedicated angler W. C. Boschen, after two years of tinkering and experiments, invented a reel with an internal drag and a handle that would turn only forward. With the help of Joe Coxe he developed the basic pattern for star-drag line winches we use today. He was so modest that he would not allow reelsmith Julius Vom Hofe to name a reel after him, instead settling for the name B-Ocean.

Oldtimers ridiculed the new gadget as overly-complicated, but criticism ceased when, in 1913, Boschen brought in the first broadbill swordfish ever caught with rod and reel, a fish weighing 355 pounds. The swordy hit a kite-trolled bait rigged by his guide, Farnsworth. Boschen was perhaps the first "stand up" big game angler, a rugged fisherman who fought his battles with only a belt socket instead of the usual fighting chair.

Aside from a few custom-made models, most of the early big game reels were crafted by Vom Hofe, but Pflueger reels also played a part. Penn and Ocean City reels were not widely used until after the Second World War.

The photo of Cliff Moore and his fish is interesting as it shows what passed for heavy tackle among less-affluent fishermen in the Depression years. His Calcutta

rapid and it went repeatedly into the air, striking from side to side, falling heavily and fighting the angler for nearly an hour."

Another marlin was captured in 1905, a third in 1908, and nine were taken in 1909, topped by C. G. Conn's 339-pounder, a very respectable striper in any year and a record at the time. Conn's guide and "gaffer" was the young and later legendary George Farnsworth. According to George Pillsbury, a pioneer angler at the island, the fish was taken from a towed skiff after being spotted by the guide during a search for tuna.

The small charter launches in use at the time, twenty-footers with ten-horsepower engines, may not have provided much feeling of security. In the early years they fished in the calm waters of the lee, close to the island, and may not have ventured far enough off-shore to encounter billfish.

It is also conceivable that there was some reluctance by boatmen and anglers to target swordfish as some believed that hooked broadbill would turn and make a ramming attack on the boat. Such attacks have occurred, but the skeptical Holder believed that the fish

Cliff Moore took this 137 pound marlin on September 5, 1936 using a solid-wrapped bamboo rod and a Pflueger reel.

bamboo rod is solidly thread-wrapped from tip to butt. Relatively inexpensive compared to laminated wood or split bamboo, rods of this type, usually mounted with a Pflueger Templar reel, were in wide use for giant black seabass, shark fishing and other rugged duty--the poor man's heavy tackle. Moore owned and operated a small charter boat, the FISHBONE, from San Pedro.

There were many capable boatmen at Avalon over the years, but none achieved George Farnsworth's towering reputation as a fish-finding expert. A great many record catches were made with his guidance. He is best remembered for his introduction of a new method of presenting a flying fish bait, suspending it from a kite so that it skipped outside the boat's wake in a natural manner. His technique with the kite led to more consistent catches than any of his contemporaries and it enabled him to pick and choose his client anglers. He discovered the Farnsworth Bank and named it after his father who brought him to the island in 1900.

When large tuna disappeared from Catalina waters in the 1930s, pursuit of marlin and broadbill became increasingly popular among those anglers dedicated to big game fishing. By then modern reels with internal drags and other tackle improvements were available, and catching big fish on light gear became the epitome of sport. In 1927 light tackle expert James W. Jump took, after a fight lasting over three hours, a 343 1/2 pound striper on 9-thread (27-pound wet test) line. This feat was surpassed in 1929 by George C. Thomas, Jr. who won a nine-hour battle with a 145-pound marlin on three-six tackle, ably assisted by captain Farnsworth. Three-six tackle consisted of a six-ounce rod six feet long and six-thread (18 pound wet test) line. Mr. Jump was also the first to boat a broadbill on 9-thread line, and the first to take two on the same day, both on 9-thread.

Then in 1930 highly skilled fisherman Robert Mankowski became the second to take a marlin on three-six, a fish of 139 pounds. He also held for many years the 9-thread striped marlin record of 348 pounds.

It was 1940 before a fisherman was able to land a broadbill and a marlin on the same day. The lucky angler was Joseph D. Peeler, guided by George Farnsworth, who performed the deed, scoring a 273-pound marlin and a 239-pound broadbill.

When catching marlin became somewhat commonplace, a few anglers turned their attention to the capture on sporting tackle of the more elusive and challenging broadbill swordfish. Famous Western novelist Zane Grey, in particular, became obsessed with catching broadbills and spent a considerable part of his fortune pursuing them. To facilitate broadbill fishing he had built an especially designed boat, the GLADIATOR. From a seat atop the mast he could observe finning swordfish and control his bait presentation. For ten years, every summer was spent at Catalina in his quest for a record catch. He took 24 swordfish from GLADIATOR and realized his goal with a 582-pound world record fish. His brother R. C. boated 18.

There is also a famous tale of an 11 1/2 hour battle with a broadbill that eventually had to be released after wearing out three strong, seasoned fishermen. At 11 A.M. on July 1, 1919, R.C. hooked the giant fish. After a desperate all-out battle, an exhausted R.C. handed off the rod to a confident Z. G. He, too, endured long hours of intense strain until at 7:30 he was forced to turn the rod over to the guide, Capt. O. J. Danielson. More struggle ensued, now in darkness. It was after 11 P.M. when the swordfish, ignoring the pressure of the dragging line, began chasing flying fish, fresh as ever. It was then that the weary anglers gave up and broke off the unbeaten monster.

In spite of his concentration on broadbill, Z. G.

was no slouch when it came to marlin. He once hung a 316-pound striper, his largest at Catalina.

In 1930 George Pillsbury was lured aside from an intensive, but mostly unproductive, pursuit of broadbill by the more accessible marlin and captured 22 spikes, followed by 28 the next year. Pretty good fishing. Before World War II, the best marlin years at Catalina were 1931 when 771 were caught, and 1940 when 401 were taken. That is a huge difference from the nine fish landed in 1909! Since records have been kept, September has always been the best month for billfishing. By 1953, a total of over 4,618 striped marlin had been brought in.

Mrs. Ganilere scored two nice albacore in 1902.

The Delight Makers

At the turn of the last century Charles Frederick Holder, the esteemed founder of the Tuna Club and early champion of rod and reel saltwater fishing, had an appropriate name for the small and medium-sized fishes he caught while exploring the sea around the Channel Islands. He called them the "Delight-Makers," a fitting appellation for the albacore, yellowtail, white seabass, and lesser fishes so abundant around the islands in those days. Already a tourist lure in the 1880s, Catalina fishing became a main attraction. Visitors indulged in the sport from a pier, skiffs or the shore and seldom without results.

While most famous for publicizing big game fishing for large bluefin tuna, Holder did not scorn the smaller species and often devoted pages of lyrical prose to the joys of pursuing them. He admired the dogged sheephead as well as the big yellowtail and 60-pound seabass that came his way.

Fishing mainly at Catalina and San Clemente Islands, he sampled all the finny favorites available. He tells of hooking huge white seabass from the beach at the Isthmus by casting a jacksmelt bait into a school of the big croakers cruising along the shore with their dorsal fins cutting the surface.

Holder was especially fond of the feisty whitefish and considered them a sort of poor man's yellowtail. Three pages of his book, *Log of a Sea Angler*, are devoted to a story of angling for whitefish at San Clemente Island, The fish ranged to 12 pounds and were taken near the surface after being chummed with lobster parts!

I have always enjoyed the photos of catches from those ancient days and recently came across a few that were new to me. They provide the quaint flavor of the times and are evidence that ordinary folk were content with ordinary fish and did not require a victorious battle with giants to find satisfaction. Today, slowed by physical limitations of old age, when angling with light tackle in calm bay waters for spotted bass and whatever else comes along, I am able to enjoy intensely my own version of the Delight Makers.

As for whitefish, they do indeed put up an excellent fight for their size. Their hard , hammering strike is easy to recognize. Today, most are caught while targeting rockfish. They go wild over shrimp, but squid is the commonest effective bait.

Beset by strong winds and rough seas, I once saved a charter trip from complete disaster by anchoring close against the lee side of South Coronado Island. In the sheltered water we could eat lunch in relative comfort. A tank of live squid had produced no yellowtail bites, but I flylined one anyway and stuck the rod in a holder. Almost at once the reel click buzzed as something took the bait with a fast run. I missed the hookset and two more before I wised up and substituted a small chunk for a whole "squirt."

A hookup resulted in a decent amount of bendo and jolting head shakes by the fish. To my surprise, a whitefish of about eight pounds proved to be the catch. I had never taken them on the surface in shallow water, nor of such respectable size. There was a school of the critters there, some weighing ten pounds, large enough to be gaffed. The passengers had great sport with them and the trip was saved. It is the only time I have encountered numbers of large whitefish right on the surface.

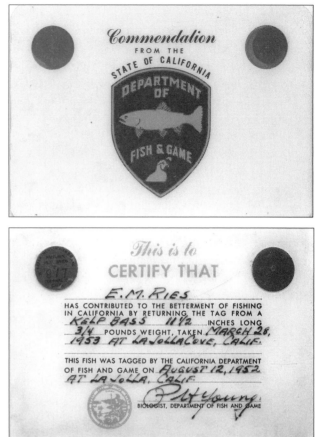

The author with a nice La Jolla bass. One of 17 taken on a half-day trip May 7, 1991.

Front and back of the Fish & Game 1953 commendation with red tags embedded.

Bass Research

In the early postwar years, an alarming decrease in the average size of kelp bass taken prompted conservation research and tagging programs by the Department of Fish & Game. In California, 3,980 bass were tagged, mostly at Catalina Island and off San Diego County. Small red plastic disks were numbered and wired through the back under the dorsal fin. By May 1953, there were 501 recoveries of tagged fish and I had taken two of them. The first was in May 1950, from the backside of Catalina when I ran a shakedown cruise with a commercial baitboat targeting barracuda and bass—at the time a legal pursuit. Fish were yanked out of the kelp with long bamboo jackpoles baited with live anchovies. The tag was turned in with information on date, location and size of the fish.

The second tagged fish came my way while sportfishing off La Jolla in March of 1953. The fish was 11.5 inches long and weighed three-quarters of a pound. After analyzing the data, the DFG sent me the tags embedded in a plastic commendation card including the date and location of the tagging nine months previous. A bulletin urging the necessity of a size limit and other info accompanied the tags.

Bass are apparently tougher than most anglers sur-

mise. To quote the bulletin: "Can kelp bass stand the strain of being caught and released? Yes! Tagging returns emphasized this. Over 500 tagged bass were returned after being caught, tagged and released. Tagged bass have been recovered that were deep hooked, bleeding, dropped on the deck, hook left in the throat; and even baked in the sun for a few minutes. Still they were again caught by somebody from 10 minutes to a year after being released."

As a result of the tagging program, the current 12-inch size limit was imposed in 1954 and, with the possession limit, has assured the continued viability of the bass fishery. Commercial landings of the desirable food fish averaged 500,000 pounds yearly in the 1920s and '30s, but declined sharply after WW II and were forbidden after 1950.

Crazy Croakers

Croakers do not get much ink in the fishing news these days, but there was a time when they were a major item in newspaper catch reports. A hundred years ago they were incredibly abundant and drew the attention of many pier and surf fishermen and the yellowfins were often pursued by boating anglers.

Spotfins grow the largest and furnished wide-open action when schooled up in "maker holes" along beaches or near piers. I enjoyed some fabulous encounters as a youngster fishing at Santa Monica. The wooden sand groine nearest the beach home of actress Marion Davies was a productive spot, as were the coastal inlets and estuaries. Mission Bay at San Diego was once famous for its spotfin fishing, but since its transformation by dredging and the huge increase in boat and watercraft traffic, there is not much doing with spotfins these days.

In the 1950s I had great luck at Imperial Beach, both in the surf and in the backwater sloughs. San Onofre was a destination for weekend campers dedicated to surf fishing in the legendary croaker holes found there. Newport's bay was also renowned for its croakers. For whatever reason, spotfins are seldom found in San Diego's big bay and after 11 years of concentrated bay fishing I have taken only one.

Spotfins favor clams, mussels, and worms for food and grow to over nine pounds in weight. The large males assume a brassy color during spawning and were called golden croakers and thought by some old-timers to be a separate species.

Yellowfin croakers are my favorites. They do not grow as large as spotfins, hut they are more colorful and aggressive. Unlike most predators, they have a mall mouth and no teeth, but they will attack a lure with ferocity. At times they can also be found in fairly deep water and l have taken them at Catalina when I was targeting barracuda.

Much more active in their pursuit of small fishes for food, they are capable of absolutely berserk behavior when they find a school of pinhead anchovies. Boiling, leaping and crashing on the surface they will annihilate a "meatball" to the last minnow. A news story dated March 30, 1911, tells of a much of larger than average yellowfin around the bell buoy in the outer San Pedro harbor. Wooden South Coast Minnows were the usual trolling lure for yellowfin croakers and the writer marveled that they were taking the large 7B Wilson spoons usually used for albacore and yellowtail. He wrote, "Several launches came in with fair box loads of four and five pounders, reporting a right jolly time of it, as the fish fought them hard and worked their light tackle very pleasingly indeed."

Spotfin croaker (Roncador stearnsii)

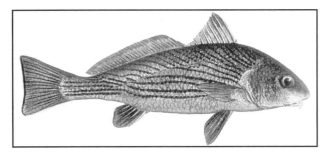
Spotfin croakers from Mission Bay, 1920s.

A Dab Here, a Dab There

In the long ago, when days grew short and surface gamefish were scarce, there was a winter alternative for more easily satisfied anglers, namely the Sanddab Specials. The trips ran mostly from the San Pedro landings. It was leisurely fishing described as an "old man's trip." Participants would often set up chairs and tables and play cards and checkers while their baits soaked on the sea bottom. Now and then they would haul in their lines, remove the 'dabs and rebait. Other than keeping it baited and free from tangles, close attention to the gear was not required.

Sanddabs are small, seldom reaching a foot in length and taking large numbers was considered essential. Experimental methods of ensuring a multiple catch on each drop were the rule. Number 6 or 8 hooks on short leaders were hung on a variety of spreaders including barrel hoops, bicycle tire rims, wire coat hangers, and handmade wire contraptions. Also used were multi-hook snagline bait catchers with a six or eight-ounce sinker on the bottom end and a two-ounce weight at the top. Pieces of cut squid are irresistible to 'dabs, but in the old days squid was not readily available on the South Coast. Small chunks of salted bait did the job. Undiscriminating mackerel were

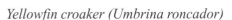
Yellowfin croaker (Umbrina roncador)

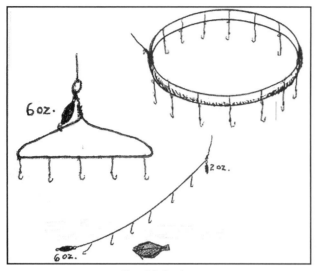

Sanddab rigs.

often taken on the 'dab rigs and tiny bits of their flesh were favorite baits.

Considered a delicacy by many, dabs are easy to fix for the frying pan by removing scales, head and guts. Little cousins to halibut, sanddabs inhabit sandy bottoms in 20 to 50 fathoms all the way from Alaska to Cabo San Lucas. Good spots exist around Catalina, the Coronado Islands and along the central coast. In the right area, sanddabs are extremely difficult to keep off the hooks. Other sea creatures find them tasty, and they are particularly good bait for lingcod.

With the rockfish season closed in 2004, a few boats in the San Francisco area run combination "crab-and-dab" trips for Dungeness crabs and target the little flatties as an option. Several boats out of 22nd St. Sportfishing in San Pedro and Pierpoint Landing in Long Beach have also resumed operating Sanddab Specials, which remain some of the most lowly and easygoing sportboat trips to be found. 'Dabs remain so plentiful that there is no limit on them.

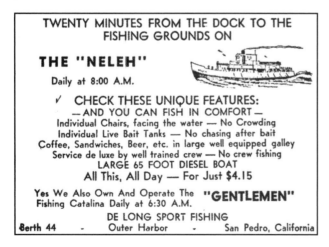
NELEH took sanddab trips.

Skipjack

Skipjack get no respect: they are the Rodney Dangerfields of tuna species. Considered a nuisance by most California fishermen, they are cursed and discarded as useless, especially when they attack jigs trolled for larger fish. It is too bad, because when fresh caught they are the most handsome of all the tunas with bright electric blue backs and beautiful iridescent pearly sides. C. F. Holder, writing almost a century ago, admired their scintillating colors and called them the "hummingbirds of the sea."

If carefully handled, skipjack are equal to yellowfin on the barbecue grill or in a can. Skipjack comprise part of the "light meat" tuna pack and no distinction is made between skipjack and yellowfin tuna by the FDA or the canneries. (Albacore are the only species legally labeled "white meat.")

In the pre-World War II years skipjack were the target of an intense fishery by commercials and sports alike and the species' appearance in local waters was welcomed. My first experience of lift pole fishing for tuna was on a Newport market boat in 1940. We caught eight-pound skipjack near the 14-Mile Bank and I found it incredibly exciting, using either a striker (squid) or bait pole.

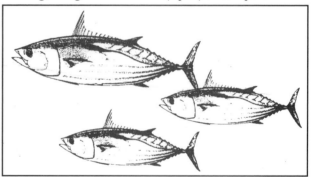

Skipjack tuna.

The secret to inducing a skippy feeding frenzy was heavy chumming with the small 3-inch sardine bait we had. As a deckhand on the sportboat VALENCIA, I remember good fishing for skipjack a mere five miles off the beach and the hard work I had scrubbing off the blood that poured from all the plump little fish bodies.

Skipjack (*Katsuwonus pelamis)* are found in tropical and subtropical seas worldwide and are the objects of a live-bait pole fishery, wherever they are found. They make up a greater percentage of the total tuna catch than any other species, especially in the large Japanese tuna fleet, and are a well-regarded and important food source everywhere, but among local sport anglers. They grow to over 30 pounds in weight, but I have seen skipjack that size only once, in the Kewalo cannery in Honolulu. If South Coast anglers encountered them in their larger sizes I am sure they would be held in more esteem.

Giant Squirts

As I write large Humboldt squid are again being taken by local anglers and the reports bring to mind my first ever encounter with the giant squirts. I was 17 and my diary says it was 23 December 1936 when my fishing pal Harold Gingerich and I arranged a tow for my skiff from the commercial bait boat QUEEN B, manned by the off-duty deckhands from the Morris Boats at Santa Monica. During the Great Depression we all were desperate to make a few more pennies for the Christmas holiday.

At 0400 we took off for Point Dume at the northwest end of Santa Monica Bay. It was a long two plus-hours boat ride before Harold and I were dropped off in the skiff. We rowed to what I thought was the Graveyard Spot, a deep rocky area off the Point, and dropped our handlines for rock cod. Armed with 20 to

We had occasional bites...

30 hooks and six-pound iron sash weights, the heavy cotton lines were baited with mackerel chunks. As we drifted on the calm sea we occasionally had bites from salmon groupers (bocaccio) and gray bass (silvergray rockfish), but disappointingly few. The QUEEN B was a mile or two away, trolling for bonito.

Around noon we felt repeated strong tugging at our baits and thought we had finally found the honey hole. Elated, we pulled the long lines hand over hand, remarking that the catch was fighting all the way, unusual with rockfish that tend to pop their swim bladders as pressure decreases.

Visions of Captain Nemo....

To our surprise and chagrin, the critters on our hooks turned out to be large Humboldt squid. They were rarely caught at that time and not a target species. We had never seen or heard of them before, but we recognized them as squid and were astonished at their size. As they surfaced they drenched us with showers of water and ink and we were in something of a panic to be rid of them. We could have cut the lines and let the weights carry them down, but were not about to give up gear that we scraped and saved to buy. I beat upon them with the gaff and Harold swatted with an oar to knock them loose from the lines. As visions of Jules Verne's Captain Nemo fighting the giant squid filled my young mind, I feared larger specimens might climb into the skiff or grab my arms. Seizing the bait knife I hacked at tentacles and hook leaders until the nasty beasts were freed and jetting away to the depths.

They have come my way a couple of times since then, but after that first encounter 74 years ago I have never had the urge to actively pursue the vicious parrot-beaked killers. They can put a bend in a rod, but I don't want to eat them, nor do I wish to be squirted with water and ink. But, if it turns you on to challenge those sea monsters, now is the time to have at 'em!

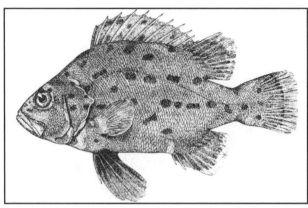

Baby giant bass are reddish in color with black spots.

Surf Surprise

A recent news story by outdoor reporter Ed Zieralski in the San Diego Union Tribune tells of a rare catch by surf fisherman Larry Hirschler at Torrey Pines State Beach, long a favorite spot for anglers. I recall the many good times I had there long ago when it was my preferred area for targeting the wily corbina.

Hirschler, 71, was using a gob of mussels on his No. 1 Eagle Claw hook attached to a 25 pound test line when he had an extraordinarily heavy strike and hookup. He chased the powerful fish up the beach as it made several long, hard runs that were close to spooling his reel. After a due amount of serious give and take, the sea beast was led into the shallows and identified as a giant black seabass, estimated by Hirschler and three other fishermen to be at least 100 pounds. After photos the fish, a protected species, was released.

A century ago giant black seabass, then called jew-fish from its resemblance to a Florida fish with that name (now goliath grouper), were incredibly abundant in Southern California and Mexican waters. The fish were slaughtered by sports and commercials alike. The adult fish were certainly edible, but required considerable butchering, and the meat was rather coarse and tough. They were generally hooked by large baits soaked on the sea bottom. Juvenile fish are often caught from sport boats and I know of several taken in San Diego Bay.

Jack Durdle with his "Mexican kelp bass."

There is on record at least one other fairly large fish captured by a surf fisherman. A 1938 brochure advertising twisted linen line by Ashaway shows a catch with the following caption: "Jack Durdle, Santa Monica, California, landed this 81-pound Mexican kelp bass by surf casting from shore, with a 9-thread (27 lb. test) Ashaway Surfman's line."

It would be surprising if the angler did not know the correct identification for the fish, but who was responsible for the incorrect ID in the caption is a mystery. It could have been someone in the advertising agency that put the brochure together, or Mr. Durdle could have made the wildly inaccurate misidentification as a joke. We will never know.

A morning's catch of 15 giant bass in Baja California by Messrs Conn, Murphy and Sharp of the Tuna Club. Such appalling slaughter was not unusual when the fish were schooled to spawn.

These 10 bass taken at Catalina on July 24, 1912 totaled 2,684 pounds. Fishing guides often targeted the big fish as easier prey for amateur anglers than large tuna or swordfish.

Novelist Zane Grey in his tackle room at home in Altadena. He probably spent more of his considerable fortune on big game fishing than any angler in history. He did exploratory fishing in Mexico, Tahiti, New Zealand and Australia in the 1920s and '30s.

Venerable angler Charles F. Holder, here at San Clemente Island, was instrumental in setting tackle standards.

Chapter 4
TACKLE AND GEAR

Tackle Classification Standards

Used to modern hi-tech gear, many anglers today are confused about the vastly different tackle of pre-World War II days. With the Catalina Tuna Club leading the way, sport tackle was standardized for purposes of competition and record keeping. Three classes were recognized: Heavy, Light and Three-Six.

Rods were usually jointed at the reel seat so the tips could be weighed. The whole rod was weighed for Three-Six. There were some slight modifications as time went on, but the basic classes endured. Bear in mind that all the rod tips were made of wood or split bamboo. Heavy tackle rod tips were to be at least five feet long and weighed not more than 16 ounces. Line was 24-thread twisted linen with a dry breaking strain of 66 pounds. No limit on reel size or length of line used for large tuna, swordfish and marlin. Light tackle tips were five feet long and nine ounces in weight. Line was 9-thread, 26 pounds dry test employed by the more skilled and daring anglers.

Three-six tackle rods were six feet long including the butt, weighing six ounces overall. Line was six-thread, 16-pound dry test. This was considered ultra-light and used on smaller game such as yellowtail and albacore. The linen lines were made from flax and were extremely fragile. Rapid rotting resulted from spots of blood or rust and they had to be dried after each use to prevent mildew. Zane Grey introduced custom made lines up to 39-thread for catching the giant marlin he pursued in the South Pacific. Wire leaders were standard for all game fish and tackle classes.

For the average, less affluent anglers fishing from piers, barges and party boats, the tackle matched individual whims but was usually in the medium 12-thread line class combined with long one-piece Calcutta bamboo rods, strong enough to bounce anything weighing up to 10 pounds.

Some remarkable catches were made by Tuna Club members using the light gear. James Jump was noted for his record catches, including a 145-pound bluefin tuna and the first broadbill swordfish on light tackle. It took extraordinary skill and patience to hook and bring to gaff those large fish on 27 pound test line.

In 1929 it took nine hours and five minutes for George Thomas, Jr. to get a permanent set in his rod fighting the first marlin taken on Three-Six tackle.

Pfishing With Pflueger

When I began ocean fishing in the early 1930s, the best reel I could hope to own was a creation of the Enterprise Manufacturing Company of Akron, Ohio. Founded in 1886 by Earnest Pflueger (pronounced Flew-ger), a German immigrant, the tackle business flourished and 30 years later claimed to be the largest fishing tackle producer in the country.

Their reels were moderately priced by Depression standards and within the reach of the average angler. Found in every sporting goods store and bait shop, they were strongly built and capable of hard usage. After saving up the proceeds from sale of the catches I made with a knuckle-buster, I was able to purchase a Pflueger Ohio, the least-expensive star drag model. It cost $6.50. If that seems hard to believe, note the price list in the 1934 advertisement appearing in Field & Stream magazine.

My first star drag reel was a Pflueger Ohio for $6.50.

The machine was heavy, but rugged, and served me well until it was lost to a thieving rascal. With the reel mounted on a Calcutta bamboo rod I conquered many yellowtail and countless barracuda, kelp bass and halibut. Eventually, a newly fashionable Penn Long Beach replaced the Ohio. Pflueger concentrated on reels of many types and the saltwater models were favorites on the South Coast. Affluent big game anglers fishing for large tuna and billfish were more apt to use the classy, but expensive Vom Hofe or J. A. Coxe reels, or if truly wealthy, the handmade winches of Arthur Kovalovsky, reelmaker to the stars.

Pflueger reels were among the first to utilize the Rabbeth and Williams external handle drags on the Templar and Oceanic models preferred by anglers specializing in the capture of giant seabass, large sharks

Pflueger Templar reel with Williams handle drag was used for heavy duty fishing.

and bat rays. Popularity of Pflueger reels began to wane in the postwar years as Penn cornered the California market with its Monofil and Jigmaster models. A few years later, unable to maintain the large share of the reel market it once enjoyed, the company went out of business. Penn reels dominated until the introduction of lightweight precision-engineered reels from Japan.

Otto Henze, founder of Penn reels, and a Senator model.

Penn Reels

After 72 years of supplying anglers worldwide with quality fishing reels, the Penn Fishing Tackle Manufacturing Company has been sold to Sea Striker Inc. in North Carolina and Master Fishing Tackle of Carson, California. Penn reels and tackle will remain in production at the three Pennsylvania facilities.

Otto Henze founded Penn in 1932 and his family has operated the business since. Otto was an avid fisherman and a toolmaker by trade. He employed his skills in creating quality reels that were simple to operate and maintain at a reasonable cost.

Originally designed for East Coast fishing, by the late 1930s Penn reels were rapidly gaining popularity on the Pacific side. Pflueger reels, with Ocean City and other brands taking a lesser share, had long dominated the trade.

I bought my first Penn reel, a Long Beach model, in 1938. It was as rugged and strongly built as Pflueger's and less expensive. After the war I purchased a model 155 Beachmaster. Its lightweight, plastic spool made it easier to cast anchovy baits and it was a huge success with live bait fishermen. A later model, the Monofil, with closer fitting tolerances and strengthened spool, corrected some of the faults of the 155s. Because Penn first offered reels that best matched current fishing techniques, it was not long before competitors faded. Many record catches were established with the reels and the company proudly claimed the title of "The Reels of Champions."

Another coup was scored in the 1950s with the introduction of the model 500 Jigmaster. With a high-speed four-to-one gear ratio it was just the ticket for California jig tossers. In spite of an annoying tendency to "eat the line," between the spool and side plate, it also became a prime general-purpose reel. The problem was later corrected with a close-tolerance aluminum spool.

In the 1970s beautifully designed graphite reels of Asian origin began to invade the market and Penn faced serious and growing competition from the newcomers. The company countered with the last word in big game fishing tackle: the superb gold-plated Internationals. Today Penn reels are still immensely popular and should remain so for years if the high quality standards of the founders are maintained.

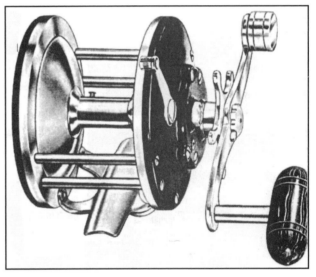

The sturdy Penn Long Beach was a favorite until replaced by the Model 500 in 1950s.

Hardware Tackle

During the hard times preceding the Second World War few sporting goods stores remained in business. There were small bait and tackle shops on or near the many piers that lined the coast, but to view a really comprehensive inventory of tackle an angler had to visit one of the hardware stores scattered through the greater Los Angeles area. Most of the city's residents did their shopping downtown in one of several big department stores such as Robinson's, Bullock's or the May Co.

For fishing tackle and outdoor equipment the place to visit was the New York Hardware Trading Company, Entz & Rucker or Carter's Hardware. These huge establishments were the equivalent of today's Home Depot or Dixieline stores. They had their own house brands and twisted linen lines such as Catalina Red Thread that were famous on the South Coast.

Check out the cost of a "complete outfit" in this ad.

Western Auto Supply also sold fishing gear and the Pep Boys even had their own reel called a Wasco. Newspaper ads on this page appeared in 1938. They reflect the deflation prices of the Great Depression and the costs of all items will astound you.

Calcutta bamboo rods were standard for ocean fishing and thrifty anglers bought the canes and fittings and did their own wrapping. The poles could be had for only 29 cents at Carter's.

In those pre-TV times there were more newspapers and every one of them had a fishing editor or columnist writing under pen names such as Jack Potts, Willy Byte and Cap'n Penny, to name a few. They gave a lot of ink to folks prominent in fishing circles. Bear in mind that the angling community was more close-knit before the postwar population explosion.

The line was not truly invisible. It was standard white linen cable twisted line with a single red strand.

All big-time hardware stores sold fishing tackle.

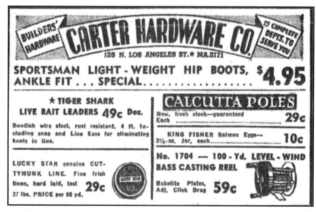
A Calcutta pole for a basic rod could be had for 29 cents.

Fishing With Wood

Over the years inventive minds have struggled to come up with surefire fish catchers. Before the age of plastics much effort was expended on wooden lures for ocean fish. Wood baits or "plugs" were useful for freshwater gamesters, but were never as successful in the salt. Most were produced by Midwestern freshwater lure manufacturers and were beefed-up versions of their best bass and musky catchers. Too light for casting with sea tackle, they were usually trolled in Pacific waters, and news reports tell of good scores of yellowfin croakers, barracuda, yellowtail, and bass taken in the early years of the last century. Zane Grey and other noted anglers used the wooden

French sailing troller. Note long outrigger poles.

Catalina Minnow and the Coast Minnow. With no built-in action, they were simply cigar-shaped painted sticks with a small propeller at the tail and a single dangling hook. The South Bend Tarp-Oreno had a scooped-out head, which gave it some action, but Grey complained that big tuna broke them up. It was not widely used.

When albacore first became a desirable commercial catch around 1910, many fishermen whittled lures out of wood and bone, but it was not long until they were replaced by factory-made cedar jigs. Every marine supply store and tackle shop stocked them until the 16-year albacore drought that began in 1926 stifled demand. I remember seeing dust-covered bins full of them and marveling at the simplicity of their design. A single lacquered, black hook jutted from an unpainted cylindrical, wooden body weighted with a lead head and eye for attaching line.

The method of manufacture is a mystery, but logic suggests the following: The unpainted cedar body was drilled through its length, pressed onto a long-shanked, eyeless hook and placed in a mold. Lead was poured around the protruding end of the hook shank, and the remainder formed into an eye. The result was a very strong, solid lure suitable for horsing in tuna on a hand-line. A few had double hooks, and there were some with

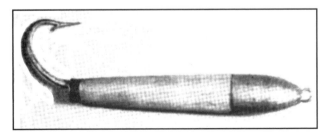

Original cedar jigs with a fixed eye were not sliders.

bone bodies. The latter were more expensive than the plain wooden jigs, and the Japanese boat-shaped bone lures were more common.

Modem versions are drilled lengthwise to slide on a leader, and many sport a coat of paint. Even without built-in action, the cedar trolling lures are effective albacore and tuna catchers to this day. Cedar jigs are said to have originated 150 years ago with the "tunny trawlers," yawl-rigged sailboats trolling the Bay of Biscay from the Brittany coast of France. On our East Coast the jigs were used for bluefish, striped bass, king mackerel, and the occasional tuna.

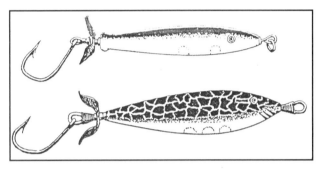

Wooden minnows were in use until about 1925.

Circle Hooks

Centuries ago, Polynesian fishermen first used handmade circle hooks fashioned from pearl shell, carved bone or wood for deepwater bottomfish. Bites were difficult to feel at the end of very long hand-lines and a self-setting hook was needed. The circle design was the answer.

Far-ranging Japanese tuna fishers eventually tried the concept on their miles of buoyed long-lines and refined the designs for metal hooks.

Until about 1970 the pattern was little known beyond Hawaii. I had encountered them at the islands in the decades after the War when my navy duty took me there. In 1972 I tried them for commercial rockfish off San Diego with outstanding success.

The only hooks available locally at the time were 7/0 and larger sizes, okay for unwary, large-mouthed rockies,

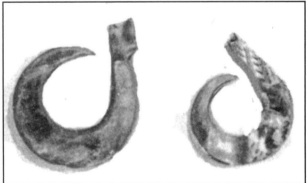

Ancient circle hooks fashioned from shell.

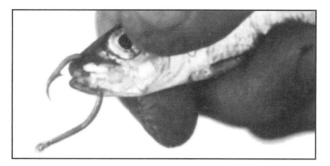

Mustad wide gap circle hook is okay for live bait.

but not suited for live-bait surface fishing. On fifty-hook handline feelers, baited with cut squid, I often brought up forty-five or more fish at a haul from 100 fathoms, the fish floating up a six-pound sinker. There were also fewer spin-offs than with the old Kirby J-hooks.

The high cost and difficulty in baiting and unhooking circles were drawbacks easily overlooked for the higher catch rate. Twenty years later I was able to find smaller circle hooks and began using them for live-bait fishing, with excellent results. The catching ability of circle hooks is well documented by scientific observation. In the late '70s a four-year study of North Pacific long-line operations using 1,400 alternate J and circle hooks, the circles produced a 63.7 percent increase in halibut catches, a 100 percent increase in sablefish and a remarkable 133.3 percent for rockfish!

The author unloading part of 1,000 pound catch of rock-fish on circle hooks, 1972.

In the six months after results were published, an estimated two million circle hooks were sold to the commercial fleet. By 1983 the entire Northern halibut fleet had switched to using the new hooks.

The setting process of circle hooks remains a mystery to many, but it is simple enough. The fish swallows the bait and swims away and the inward-curved hook does not stick anywhere in its mouth until a tightened line pulls it into a corner of the jaw. The tension pulls the head back as the body continues forward, pushing the hook point out and around the jawbone. It is important to put the reel in gear and let the line come taut, then make a slow sweep with the rod to set the hook which will always be in the corner of the mouth. The customary sharp yank on a rod for ordinary hookset will only jerk a circle hook out of the fish's mouth.

It has taken a few years for the circle hook model to gain wide acceptance by sport fishermen. The first hooks marketed had narrow gaps and were hard to handle, bait and unhook from a catch. In recent years all major hook manufacturers have produced circle hooks in varieties suitable for sportfishing, including wider gaps for easier baiting and smaller wire diameters for less weight, an important feature when using live bait.

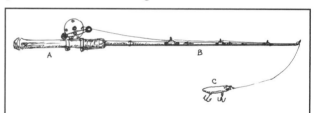

My improvised rod, reel and plug for largemouth bass.

Improvisation

In 1935 I was a callow 16 years of age and already a dedicated fishing fanatic. Outdoor magazines of the time had plenty of fishing stories and I read them all, but was frustrated because freshwater species got most of the ink. The few salt water stories were all East or Gulf Coast oriented. Largemouth bass fishing was, however, a subject in nearly every issue, and I yearned to experience that popular pastime.

My chance came when a cousin, who had an avocado ranch in Escondido, invited my family for a weekend visit. He mentioned that bass fishing at Lake Hodges was available. Assembling suitable tackle became urgent, and my funds were very limited in those Depression days.

To build a bait-casting rod for minimum expense, I went to Volke's Bait and Tackle Shop on Santa Monica Pier. The shop had racks of long yellow cane and nodeless brown Calcutta bamboo. Poles were trimmed with a hack-

Cheap casting reels like this could be had for as little as 69 cents in the Depression years.

saw to customers' specifications and many cut off pieces were lying about. I was able to pick up a short butt piece of yellow cane and light tapering wand from the tip of a Calcutta pole. The tip piece was about 4 ½ feet in length and less than ¼ inch in diameter at the small end.

Next day I took the two pieces to the high school woodshop and drilled out one end of the butt piece and jammed the wand into it along with some wood glue. Next, I purchased three small guides and a tip and wrapped them to the long section. I picked up a low-end baitcast reel for 75 cents and secured it to the rod butt with hose clamps. A 50-yard spool of six-thread (18 pound test) linen line was spooled, and I lacked only some suitable lures. These I fashioned from broom handle pieces shaped and tapered on the woodshop lathe. For wobble action the heads were scooped out with a chisel. Screw eyes and treble hooks were attached, red and white paint applied, and I had a pair of bass plugs.

Two test the new rod, I joined a group that after school paddled to the breakwater in a skiff. In the bucket of live bait bummed from a returning sport boat, I found a 6-inch sardine. Using a wire leader and forged book, I flylined the 'dine on the outer side of the rocks. I hooked and landed a 6-pound calico bass, my largest fish taken from the breakwater. It was an excellent workout for my makeshift rod.

My dad and I took a rental skiff at the lake, and I cast my plugs near the shoreline structures. Several bass boiled on the lures, but I got no hookups. We were running out of time when I begged one more stop under the highway bridge crossing the lake. I found a spinner among the junk in Dads tackle bag and tied it on, adding a couple of split shot for weight. One more cast and it was time to go. The spinner was dropped by a concrete piling, and the retrieve induced a smashing strike. Up came a nice 3- pound largemouth bass, my first ever. Thrilled and inspired, after a couple

more casts, I hooked another fish of the same size. Shortly after, we were in the parking lot boarding our car when a passerby offered to buy my fish for 50 cents. Elated, I accepted the offer and my excursion with improvised tackle had a happy and satisfactory ending.

Survival Fishing

In the dark early days of World War II many survivors of sunken ships adrift on the seas perished from thirst and hunger before they were rescued. Researchers found that almost all saltwater fish could be eaten raw and that drinkable fluid could be squeezed from fish flesh wrapped in cloth.

Under the guidance of famous angler Michael Lemer, a group of big-game fishermen gathered to devise and test a fishing kit with which lifeboats and rafts could be equipped. The kits quickly became standard for all U.S. vessels. Collector Jim Ziegler recently found a kit and kindly sent me photos and a copy of the instructions that came with it.

During my wartime sojourns in the Solomon and Marshall Islands in the tropical Pacific, I fished whenever opportunity and duty permitted. I was aware my ship's life rafts had kits, but tampering was strictly forbidden and severely punished. Although I would have dearly loved access to the tackle, I was never able to use a kit and had to make do with whatever makeshift gear I could fashion myself or buy ashore. As a boat coxswain I had somewhat more opportunity to wet a line than most of my shipmates.

Ziegler's photos show the kit was an apron-like cloth with pockets for the handlines wrapped on wooden H-frames, and various lures, and hooks. Most of the lures were familiar trolling feather jigs of the kind imported in

Contents of the survival fishing kit.

prewar years from Japan and used mainly for albacore and bonito. Because it could be stored for long periods, pork rind for bait was also provided in the kits.

Tackle expert and author Harlan Major also assembled donated sportfishing gear of all types and sent packets to servicemen in all theaters for recreational fishing. I surely wish I had known of it when I was on Eniwetok Atoll and had more opportunities to fish after the tide of war rolled westward. A letter would no doubt have produced results. A very complete account of the tackle kits development and the effects of the war on fishing is to be found in Mike Rivkin's excellent illustrated book *Angling and War*.

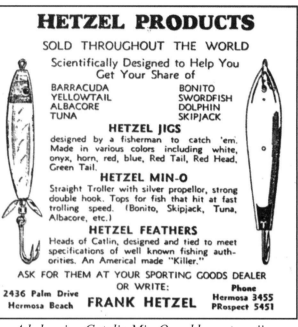
Ad showing Catalin Min-O and bone-type jig.

Plastics Pioneer

Bakelite, an early plastic used for sideplates on cheap reels, was either black or brown and extremely brittle. When Bakelite's 1910 patent expired in 1927, the Catalin Corporation began producing a similar material. A new method allowed them to add 15 colors to the available range. Catalin replaced the wood and steel in many products, making them much more affordable, an important feature during the Great Depression.

Ardent angler Frank Hetzel of Hermosa Beach was one of the first entrepreneurs to apply the new technology to the manufacture of fishing lures. As early as 1935, he produced copies of Japanese whalebone jigs, wooden Coast Minnows ,and heads for feather jigs in Catalin hard plastic. The material differed from Bakelite in its strength and capacity to absorb colors. In addition to other hard Catalin lures, he fashioned a few items in rubber , such as a flying fish and a squid imitation.

Ad in outdoor magazines in 1943 shows the kit apron and Lerner and crew working on the kits.

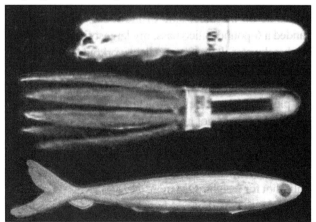

Hetzel trolling lure, rubber squid and flying fish.

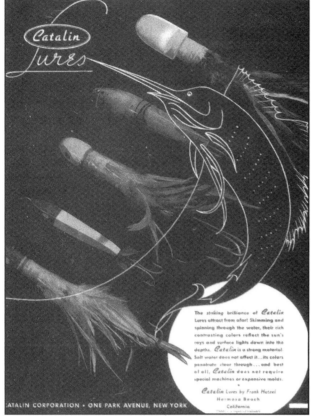

Ad showing Catalin jig heads.

Hetzel appears in my collection of newspaper clippings in 1938 and was apparently well known in fishing circles by that time. The next mention that 1 could find was in "Capt. Penny's" column in the Daily News on May 23, 1940: "Frank Hetzel manages to get two or three bluefin on every trip to San Diego, but of course he gets them on hump-backed white bone jigs with green tails--those things rarely miss."

I was able to examine one of the bone jig imitations from the collection of Mike Farrior and it has a light yellowish color with a patch of red at the tail of its typically boat-shaped body. A metal reinforcing plate is set in the nose to take the strain of the wobble ring and the name "HETZEL" is stamped on the flat side. The method of securing the hook is unique. Instead of a screw or rivet through the hook eye, the Hetzel has a long eyeless hook shank turned down in a short 90 degree angle to fit snugly into a hole drilled through the jig. The heavy wire fastening the after end was soldered to the hook shank, another innovation. The whole rig was very strong and suitable for trolling, but its light weight would make casting difficult.

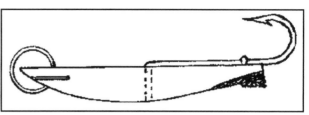

Hetzel's imitation bone jig.

Some Old Time Lures

Jig casters now choose between two basic types of very affective lures for saltwater fish: metal or plastic. Both are easily castable with modern tackle. In the pre-World War II era there were few lures suitable for cast-and-retrieve sea fishing as most reels of the day had heavy metal spools wound with sticky linen line. A simple plated torpedo sinker with a treble hook dressed with a few feathers worked well enough when fish were abundant. There were lures of wood, metal, feathers and horsehair, mostly designed to be trolled and without enough intrinsic weight to cast. The Wilson spoon is an example of a lightweight trolling lure, intended for salmon, but effective on all game fish.

Bone and feather jigs are usable on rod and reel if trailed behind a sinker, but awkward to use in that fashion. An aluminum copy of a bone jig was a killer, but still too light for easy casting. Several of the Eastern manufacturers introduced models similar to fresh water bass plugs that were largely ineffective in Pacific waters. Around 1930 the Dodger and a few others of castable weight were introduced, but only the Dodger gained favorite status. The original Dodger was 3.1 ounces in weight and had a satin nickel coat. Around 1938 it was supplanted with a new 2.4 ounce model that was cast from pot metal, and plated with shiny chrome crossed by a painted red stripe. Both were deadly gamefish killers.

In the 1950s lures of hard plastic and rubber began to appear, gradually supplanted with the superior "iron" and soft plastics we have today. Herewith a few examples of old jigs and lures that were in use on the local ocean.

Original Dodger had plenty of weight for casting.

Left: This thing had no trade name that I know of and no built-in action. It was plated lead with red glass eyes and sometimes it caught a lot of barracuda.

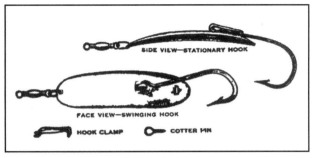

The Wilson spoon was designed as a salmon trolling lure, but it worked well for all game fish.

Weirdest was O.C. Tuttle's Deep Sea Devil Bug, a trolling lure fashioned from hair wrapped on a 9/0 hook. Feathers did it better.

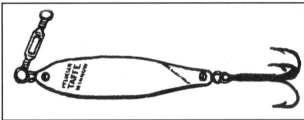

Pflueger's Taffe jig was four inches long and weighed a heavy four ounces. Very castable, but with limited action, it was never widely popular in California.

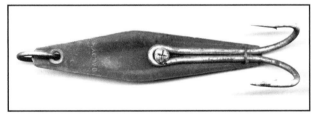

Famous Baldy jigs were hard plastic copies of successful bone lures This model was green with a red belly patch and was a good albacore catcher.

The Streamline Dodger replaced the original in the late 1930s and is still found in a few tackle boxes.

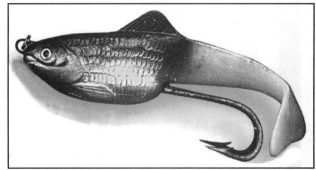

French-made Vivif rubber "toad" was briefly popular in the 1950s as a bull calico bass catcher.

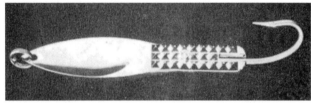

The postwar Spoofer had enough weight to cast, but its action was not as attractive as the old Dodger.

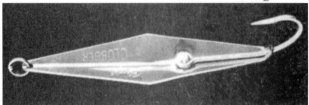

Clyde's Clobber in the 1950s was too hard to cast, but had nice action and could catch fish. There are some similar models still in limited use.

The Greatest Change

What is the most significant change in fishing since the old days? That is the question I am most often asked. There have been many, but the most important, in my opinion, is the introduction of synthetic lines.

Nothing has improved an angler's ability to fool and hook fish like nylon monofilament. For thousands of years fishermen used vegetable fibers or animal sinews to present their baits. Before DuPont chemists invented nylon in 1938, the best line for rod and reel anglers was made of twisted linen threads. In new condition it was incredibly strong for a plant fiber, but was also extremely vulnerable to rot and damage from a variety of causes. A tiny drop of blood, a rust stain, fish slime, or prolonged exposure to sunlight were all destructive.

If the line was put away wet, it was susceptible to mildew, another harmful factor. Line dryers were a vital piece of equipment for dedicated sea anglers. If a dryer was unavailable, the line could be stripped from the reel in loose coils and sprinkled with salt to accelerate drying.

Fishing lines made of twisted nylon strands were tried in 1939, but were limp, loosely laid and easily tangled.

Their strength and durability were recognized, but they made no real impact on the market until after World War II. Parachute canopies and shroud lines of nylon were among the primary uses of the stuff during the war.

In 1947 monofilament was launched as a substitute for silkworm gut leader material. It was stiff and brittle, but more transparent and stronger than gut and it found immediate favor with anglers. At the same time, nylon fibers were fashioned into multifilament braided lines for use on reels. Some were flat and ribbonlike, coated with a wax and dyed green. They were a sensation. Strong and impervious to blood and damp, it was no longer necessary to dry them after each use.

In 1953, I first used a nylon leader on braided nylon line to catch yellowtail and still have these leaders in my collection. They were sold under the Sevenstrand brand, a company that had for many years successfully marketed packaged wire leaders. It did not take long before monofilament replaced wire leaders for all types of salt water fishing except jig-casting for barracuda and trolling for billfish and sharks.

In 1957 I first rigged my commercial albacore trolling jigs with 90-pound test monofilament leaders and outfished my "buddy boat" by a ratio of five to one. He was using the old style three-foot wire leaders.

By 1957 improvements in chemistry and manufacturing produced nylon monofilament suitable as main line for use on reels. Now an angler's entire line could be a leader! With its use catches of all game fish increased dramatically and it remains the standard today.

Next came the "braids" under the generic name of Spectra. Nearly impervious to rot, incredibly strong for its diameter and with practically no stretch it, is the main

This 1957 ad shows monofilament lines were in general use.

line of choice for most serious anglers today. The lack of stretch makes it extremely sensitive to every wiggle of a live bait and tiniest tentative nibble of a wary fish.

The latest advance in technology is fluorocarbon monofilament, said to be invisible to finicky fish, and with continued refinements I predict it will become the new standard for main line or leader topshots on Spectra. Greater strength for smaller diameters and increased flexibility and softness to inhibit backlashes seems to be the present aim of manufacturers.

I first used these leaders for yellowtail in 1953.

In 1930s a complete outfit: rod, reel and line, for $8!

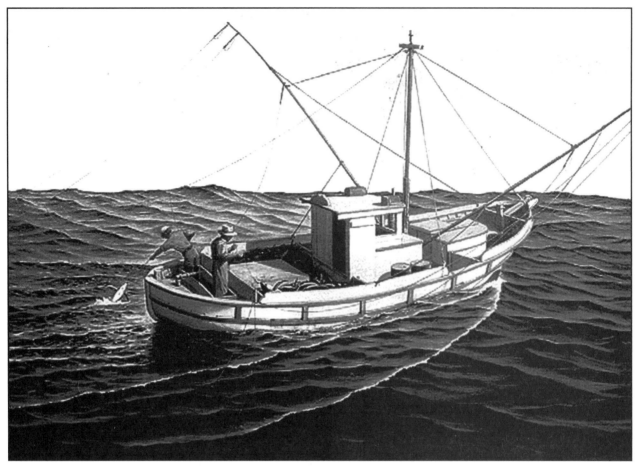

A typical Monterey trolling for albacore in the early 1920s. From a painting by the author.

The dark bait tanks on these albacore boats at Fish Harbor were painted 'Tuna Red." Canvas covered lampara bait nets on the stern and bundled lift poles are visible, c. 1925.

Chapter 5
COMMERCIAL FISHING

Trolling for Albies

Bob Franko's article on tuna trolling in the June 2004 issue stirred memories of my days of commercial albacore fishing. Spreading the lines with outrigger poles was standard practice and remains so today. The difference was the boat continued moving at a steady speed and every line was a "meat line" pulled in by hand. Nowadays the fish are winched in on "pie-plate" mechanical pullers that eliminate the hard labor of pulling by hand.

Until the late 1950s leaders were wire attached to 72-thread hard laid cotton cord. Some trollers tapered their lines a bit with green linen, or braided nylon after it became available. I first used monofilament leaders in 90 to 100-pound test in 1957 and caught more fish than my "buddy-boat" who stuck with wire.

Lines were in staggered lengths, ranging from a 20-fathom mast line to short lines of two fathoms, sometimes less. Small trollers usually had three or four lines on each outrigger and two or three from the boat's stem. Large boats had as many as 14 lines. Some were weighted, and these deep lines often carried bone or plastic wobblers. The others dragged feather jigs.

Colors and patterns were a matter of a fisherman's individual preference. Some used tinned lead heads from Japan with all-white feathers, while others preferred the plastic heads that appeared after the Second World War. The lead heads had embedded red glass eyes or pieces of abalone shell. Heads and packages of feathers in various colors were sold at marine hardware stores. I spent many winter evenings overhauling jigs, wrapping on new feathers, sharpening the double hooks, etc.

Jig color was and still is a matter of controversy, but I agree with Franko that color is less important than how the lure moves in the water and appears to the fish. I have seen many albacore caught on outlandish-looking jigs that certainly bear not even the slightest resemblance to anything in nature. The efficiency of cedar jigs is well known, and they look like nothing but a stick of wood. They have been catching albacore in European waters for centuries, so they must have an instinctive appeal to the fish.

Gone is the huge fleet of small one-and two-man trollers that once plied the sea off the California coast, supplying the raw material for bustling canneries in San Diego and San Pedro.

Modern commercial albacore trollers can fish year around in the mid-Pacific and deliver their catches at Samoa and Hawaii. To see their large, seaworthy boats visit the Commercial Basin near G Street in San Diego. There are not many left.

Tuna Red

Zane Grey was cruising the Catalina Channel in search of his obsession, broadbill swordfish, and complained bitterly about the commercial albacore boats "dashing to and fro in pursuit of every splash of breaking fish." He wrote that everywhere he looked, red spots were visible. For whatever reason, probably to make the spattering of fish blood less apparent, the bait tanks and inboard bulwarks of the commercial boats were uniformly painted a color known as "Tuna Red." C. J. Hendry Company, the major ship chandler and source of supplies for the fishing fleet, sold it under their own house brand.

Immigrant Japanese fishermen, using techniques known to them for centuries, were foremost in the development of live-bait fishing for albacore. A large colony formed at San Pedro and on Terminal Island around Fish Harbor, site of the new canneries. The color scheme of their boats was predominantly a white hull with black trim and red interior. The theme was usually preserved when albacore boats were bought and converted for sportfishing. Such conversions were simple and easy, requiring only the addition of bench seating, pipe-and-chain lifelines, a head and a box of cork lifejackets. The Santa Monica boats that I remember from my first fishing ventures in the 1930s all had the same paint jobs. It was not until much later, when purpose-built sport boats began to appear, that new color schemes were seen.

Fishermen from Mediterranean countries favored a hull trimmed with other color mixes, the Italians' favorite being an accent of bright blue. Large purse seiners often had black hulls, and in San Diego I saw a number of boats with green and gray hulls.

The once-flourishing fleet of small commercial boats is a thing of the past and most of those remaining are salmon trollers on the North Coast. The canneries are gone, and attacks by environmentalists, increasing restrictions and the high cost of operations have made it nearly impossible for a single independent fisherman to make a living from the sea.

Tools for Tuna

The 2009 year was an excellent season for tuna, dorado, and yellowtail. Sadly, it was beyond my physical capacity to participate, but I have my memories of other

Method of rigging two poles to one leader and hook.

good years. I recall the days when a fleet of large, sturdy commercial boats ventured thousands of miles from California ports in search of tuna for the hungry canneries.

In the time before the Second World War and the invention of synthetic twine, the fishing was done most effectively with hook and line and live bait. "Tuna clippers" were developed from the small local albacore chasers that first supplied the canners. A key to profitable large catches was the fast pace of the fishing when a biting school of tuna was found.

When the fish came aboard, the almost instant hook release was due to the lure used. Japanese fishermen, after much experimentation, developed the "brass pipe squid," basically, a lead-filled brass tube with a near-right angle barbless hook embedded, and the lure is dressed with white feathers that undulate when moved in the water. Tuna chummed to a feeding frenzy will readily bite the lure. When yanked aboard, a little slack in the line allows the leverage of the weighted head to easily dislodge the hook. Skillful fishermen can unhook small tuna while the fish are still in the air with a short flip of the pole that momentarily slacks the line.

The stout imported Japanese cane poles were cut to a length of about nine or ten feet, and the nodes were usually filed down somewhat. A becket, or loop, of heavy cord a half-inch or greater in diameter was

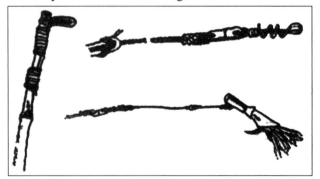
Method of rigging poles for tuna fishing. Not to scale.

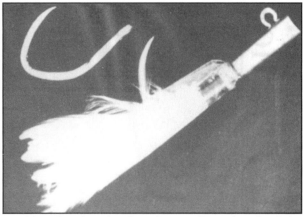

Barbless live bait hook and "squid" or "striker" for tuna.

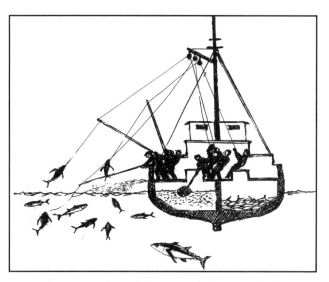

Diagram shows European fishing method.

secured to the end of the pole with wraps of twine. The becket prevented the line from wrapping around the pole while fishing. The heavy tanned cotton line was secured to it with a becket bend, a strong knot easily untied for adjusting length.

For one-pole fishing, a pigtail swivel was spliced to the line and the steel wire leader with lure or bait hook attached. To prevent kinking, the wire was usually in two parts, Large tuna required multipole sets with lines bridled to a single hook. The bridle consisted of a special heavy bronze ring with three to five swivels attached, one of which had a pigtail connector for the leader.

European Tuna Fishing

For those curious about the exciting old-time method of commercial tuna fishing with hook and line, it may be of interest to know that a similar fishery still exists in the Eastern Atlantic. As carried on by French, Portuguese and Spanish fishermen, the method is old-fashioned and labor intensive. A few modern techniques are employed, such as sprayed water to excite the tuna and fiberglass poles in place of the old wood and bamboo.

Fishing is done from a boat's deck instead of from outboard platforms such as the "racks" used on American tuna clippers. Small tuna under 30 pounds ("one-pole" size) are thrown aboard with short poles, as in American boats. Poles on our boats averaged about ten feet in length, with some individual variations. For boating larger fish lines were bridled together in two, three and four-pole sets. The big tuna could still be hauled aboard by a multipole team using barbless lures that released instantly and were returned to the water immediately.

On European boats, larger tuna are taken with bait presented on a line longer than the pole, which might be 12 to 15 feet in length. A topping lift is attached to the pole near the tip and led through a block fixed to a horizontal jackstay behind and above the fishermen. A feathered "striker" or "squid" is too difficult to move in an enticing manner with

the long lines and poles attached to topping lifts, so live bait is preferred. When a fish is hooked, the pole man lifts and is aided by a backup man hauling on the topping lift. When the pole is vertical the fish is still in the water, but within reach of a third man, the gaffer, who sticks the tuna in the head and hauls it aboard, assisted by the topping lift man if necessary. The method is slow and labor intensive compared to American or Japanese methods of pole fishing, but European fishermen manage respectable tonnage nevertheless. It is possible the fish in those waters are too spooky to readily rise to the surface on chum and will only bite on deep bait. It may also be that live bait is so difficult to catch in quantity that high volume chumming to generate a surface frenzy is not customary.

Below is a scene of pole fishing on a small French tuna boat. From left to right: First man is gaffer handling fish for the pole and lift team to his left. The next team of

57

Spanish live bait tuna fishing. Note long fiberglass poles and slack topping lifts. Lines are too long for fish to be lifted over the rail with poles.

MARY ANN.

three has enough lift to snatch a fish clear of the water. The third team of three has a large tuna head-out that will have to be gaffed. Note jackstay with blocks rigged for pole topping lifts. Lines and leaders are longer than the poles so that a gaffer is needed to get the fish aboard. When a tuna is hooked, one man hauls the line to help the pole reach vertical, bringing the fish within reach of the gaffer. Thus it takes three men to boat a tuna that American fishermen would catch more quickly with a two-pole set. Long, stout pole off mast is a trolling outrigger. This same basic commercial fishing method is also used on Portuguese and Spanish tuna boats.

Last of the Longliners

Hook and line commercial fishing from small one-man boats based in San Diego is a thing of the past. One of the last practitioners of the ancient longline method was Joe DeSanti who passed away at age 82 in December 2005. For more than 40 years he plied the sea in his 32-foot Monterey boat LA DIANA, setting hundreds of baited hooks for sculpin, rockfish and hali-

but. Longline rigs were most often used as anchored setlines for bottom fish and occasionally as midwater drift lines for mackerel. The method is also used by Newport dory fishermen.

Joe's partner was Tony Giacalone in his sister boat MARY ANN. The fishing friends persisted in a centuries-old, labor-intensive, style of fishing once employed by hundreds of independent fishermen along the coast. For many years the partners regularly supplied a major seafood restaurant with a continuous supply of tasty sculpin and other bottomfish.

I made some of my own first ventures into market fishing with a longline, usually called a setline in Santa Monica, in 1935. Learning to safely and rapidly handle the hundreds of hooks and the fish they dredged up was a skill I was proud of. Let the reader bear in mind, I write of a desperate time when sport and commercial fishing often blended and many anglers sold their catches.

LA DIANA.   *Right: Unloading longlined sculpin.*

Tinned 6/0 kirby hooks, each attached to a leader of cotton seine twine, were tied to a main line at intervals. The tanned line was coiled into flat wicker baskets with pieces of cork fastened to the edges. As they were baited with salted anchovies or cut mackerel, hooks were placed in the cork rim.

Once at the chosen spot the boat cruised slowly as anchor and buoy were put overboard and lines were set in a continuous string. With the aid of a stick, coils and hooks were lifted from the basket and flipped over the side. Another anchor and buoy were tied to the end of the line. When the set was completed, the first buoy was picked up and the line retrieved. Fish were removed as the line came in and was recoiled in the baskets.

Longline fish were once a major source of fresh market fish in California, but as the small boats dwindled in number, netted fish have supplanted hook-caught fish and most of the product is sold frozen. A highly-regulated mechanized form of longlining with much heavier gear is still used for northern halibut and black cod.

Rockfish and sheephead are two of the species captured for the live fish market.

Bring 'em Back Alive

Imagine sportfishing for readily catchable species and being able to sell everything caught for prices high enough to make a modest living. Two new rod-and-reel commercial fisheries have as recently as 1992 been developed in central California. One involves catching and delivering alive a variety of shallow water rockfish. The other is for barred surfperch.

The state's growing population of quality-conscious Asian seafood fanciers provides the market and the high prices that make the labor-intensive enterprises work. The commercial fishing journal *National Fisherman* reports that rod-and-reelers from Oxnard to Morro Bay are delivering up to 15,000 pounds of live fish weekly. Fishermen receive up to $3.50 a pound for live fish, but only $1 for the dead. By delivering directly to restaurants and markets, a few fishermen with their own tank trucks make much more.

Deflating their swim bladders is the key to keeping rockfish alive. Their bodies are pierced with a hypodermic needle, allowing the expanded gas to escape. If this is done properly and immediately when fish are boated, rockfish will swim to the bottom of the tank and rest quite comfortably.

Shallow water species are targeted as the large individuals from deep water are beyond saving alive when brought to the surface. Fishing is usually done in water less than 100 feet deep. Prime species that live well in tanks are brown rockfish, gopher rockfish and black and yellow rockfish. Other desirables are sheephead and cabezon.

Nobody knows why, but some types live better than others. Kelp, blue and vermillion rockfish (reds) expire quickly while sheephead live up to two weeks.

Tackle is simple. Two J-hooks on a 25-pound test gangion with a torpedo sinker are attached to a standard rod and reel. Bait is cut squid. To keep from putting extreme stress on rockfish by winding up too fast, low gear ratio reels are the best. A quick hookset on the first nibble is required to prevent gut-hooking. Lip-hooked fish need less handling and live better.

When the weather is good and the fish are biting, it isn't unusual for four men to catch 300 pounds of live rockfish in a day, plus additional numbers that die. Catching the fish is the easy part.

Careful handling of the catch to insure survivability, and getting it delivered to the buyer, are the hard parts. Customers at the Chinese restaurants that feature live product claim that there is no finer gourmet food than fish that are dressed just before cooking. They select the individual they wish prepared and in less than ten minutes the steam-cooked fish is ready to eat. Now that is fresh fish!

A lesser enterprise is the catching and selling of barred surfperch. The fishing is mostly north of Morro Bay as it is illegal in the southern counties. Light sportfishing tackle is used with a variety of natural and artificial bait. Roaming the beaches, the fishermen cast to likely spots. The catch is usually carried in back packs and must be checked and certified by Department of Fish & Game officials before being marketed. Most of the catch is sold to buyers in the L.A. area. The limited number of fishermen who participate do so for supplemental income. They do not rely on perch for a living. At least one former San Diego sportfishing skipper indulges in the commercial surf fishing, but I suspect he dabbles more for the fun of it than for the money.

Commercial fishing with rod and reel has been tried sporadically over the years in specialized fisheries. Compared to net fishing production can only be measured in pounds rather than tons of saleable fish. A few rods and reels were found on commercial boats when it was legal to sell kelp bass, although long cane jackpoles and handlines were the usual gear for fishing in the weeds. For deepwater rockfish heavy duty rods with monel wire lines were used, mostly for exploratory drops. Thousands of fish were sold by sport boat crews and anglers in the 1930s. It was legal if the fisherman had a $10 commercial license.

With gillnets on the way out it is gratifying to see the revival of hook and line commercial fishing. It is unlikely that such a selective, low volume method will ever result in destructive overfishing.

Private boaters my be tempted to try saving live rockfish for their own table fare. If so, have at it, but don't attempt to sell your catch unless you have a valid commercial license for your boat and every fisherman aboard.

Doyle and Putters

In the early 1930s when I broke into the fishing game in Santa Monica Bay, Jim Putters of Redondo was a well-known and respected commercial fisherman. In the early years of the 20th Century he persevered in his vocation and location and attained legendary status. Every method of hook-and-line fishing from small boats was tried and he was credited with introducing the poke-pole technique for catching barracuda and fashioning trolling jigs that were so sought after that they eventually were factory made and sold to others.

"Putters poke-poles a tuna from the MARLIN II," from a painting by the author.

Chet Doyle peddling a catch of chili pepper rockfish on Redondo Pier.

Chester Doyle, in 1926 a recent high school graduate, found work peddling fish on the Redondo pier and as a sportboat deckhand and helper for Putters and other fishermen. For 25% of the proceeds, he sold the catch on the pier and a fisherman could go home and rest up for the next long day on the sea. Chili pepper rockfish brought 15 to 25 cents each and halibut, bass, barracuda and yellowtail were sold by the pound or piece. The chilis were known at Redondo as "johnny cod."

Chet kindly shared his stories and photos of those days with me when we corresponded in 1988. He wrote, "I was working with Jim Putters on his boat MARLIN. We were fishing for rock cod at the time. For a few mornings we had seen swordfish. They would come clear out of the water and flip over backwards, just playing, it seemed. We put out a 300-hook setline for rock cod and were waiting for fish to get on the line."

"I was watching another boat a couple hundred yards from us, He was pulling his line and seemed to be in trouble. Finally, he threw it all in the water and pulled over to us. He said, "I must be hooked to a whale, or something that big. It jerked the line right out of my hands!"

Jim Putters' boat MARLIN ready to unload a box of rockfish, 1926. Chet Doyle has the long gaff in hand.

"Jim had a rifle for shooting sharks when they gave us trouble, so he went over to see if we could help. We finally got it to the surface and it was a broadbill swordfish. Jim shot it and we were able to get it across the stern of the boat and took off for shore in high spirits.

The fish was weighed on the pier at 310 pounds. It was the first of five we caught that summer—all the same way, tangled up in rock cod lines. They would eat the hooked fish and get all wrapped up and become almost helpless."

"Another time I was working with a man in an 18-foot outboard skiff setting the line on the bottom near shore for halibut. A school of yellowtail swam by, so close to the surface we could see them clearly. This guy quickly pulled part of the line up and attached some old life preserver corks to keep it near the top. Then he put several fresh anchovies on each hook and we were kept busy running up and down the line to where the corks were bobbing."

"There were several fish on at once and we lost quite a few, but before they left the bottom of the skiff was covered with nice big yellowtail, around 30, I think."

Salmon, Anyone?

Anglers fishing from Santa Barbara north sometimes see in season commercial boats trolling for salmon. Since the demise of pole fishing for tuna this hook-and-line method is the one closest to sportfishing. It began over 100 years ago when sailboats dragged a handline or two in Monterey Bay.

By 1904 there were 175 sailboats trolling in the bay, but only three with gasoline engines. Conversion to gas engines proceeded over the next dozen years and the use of outrigger poles to spread multiple lines became general.

King salmon are often erratic and unpredictable in their movements and occasionally are caught as far south

Chester Doyle shows off two big yellowtail.

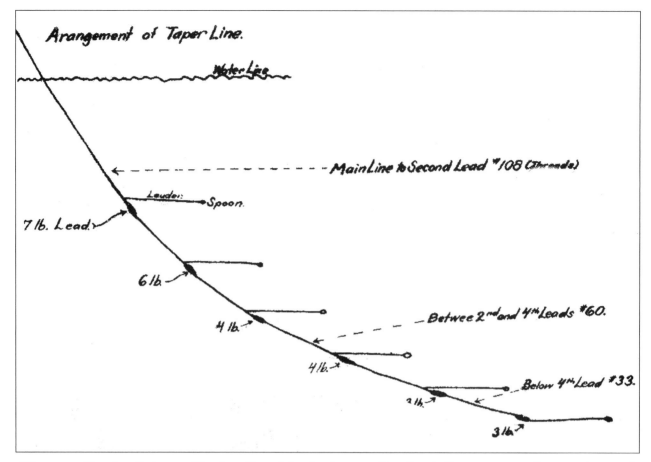

Diagram of hand pulled, rope-like, heavily weighted salmon trolling line before power gurdies were invented.

as Newport Beach. In 1947 I took one on a bone jig while trolling for white seabass and barracuda off Ballona Creek, now the site of Marina Del Rey.

Schools were often in deep water so long, tapered, heavily weighted cotton lines trailing two to six lures were used. The weights were distributed along the line as shown in the diagram.

All pulling was done by hand and it was backbreaking work. Imagine hauling hand over hand from a moving boat a line that carried up to 40 pounds of lead sinkers with a thrashing 30-pound fish at the end. It was so hard on hands that fishermen wore special circular grooved rubber "clinchers" to grip the lines.

There was little change in the method until the late 1930s when "gurdies" came into use. These mechani-

Some early salmon trolling spoons.   *At Monterey sailing fishboats trolled for salmon.*

Power gurdies for wire lines and cannon ball weights.

cally powered reels spooled with stainless wire lines greatly improved the catch rate and eliminated much of the heavy labor. The weight was on the end of the line instead of along its length and it hung at a more vertical angle than the cotton lines. At intervals above the sinker lures on short leader lines were attached to the wire with removable snaps. Along with a number of sophisticated refinements, this is the basic method in use today. Although hundreds of trollers still work in Alaska and the Northwest, the number of California boats is rapidly dwindling.

Modern salmon troller. Davit support fairlead blocks for wire lines from gurdies.

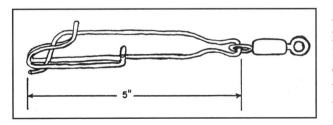

Snap used to attach leader and lure to the wire trolling line.

Boating a trolled salmon.

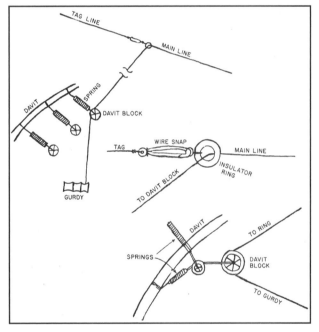

Drawing shows method of rigging trolling gear. An improved "clothespin" gadget has replaced the porcelain insulator on the ends of outrigger pole tag lines.

First Purse Seiner

Aside from salmon, sardines were the primary species used for canning in the 19th century and the port of San Pedro got its first cannery when the California Fish Company opened in 1893. One of the owners was Alfred P. Halfhill whose later experiments with packing albacore founded the canned tuna industry. To provide the sardines the ALPHA, first purse seine boat in California, was built in Alameda. She was a 22-ton sloop-rigged vessel with a 60-foot mast for sailing and was also fitted with a newfangled gasoline

ALPHA, a little the worse for wear, ready to unload.

engine, probably the first ever in a Southern California boat. So primitive was the engine that a shotgun shell was loaded in a special cylinder and hit with a hammer to provide starting ignition. If there was sufficient breeze cruising was done under sail and the engine was fired up for the net-setting maneuvers. A skiff, or tender, was towed and released with the end of the seine when a set was made. The skiff helped to support the bag of concentrated fish while they were scooped aboard the larger vessel.

The seven man crew consisted of captain, engineer, cook and four deckhands. They earned a wage as

A hand windlass lifts the brailer as it scoops sardines from the bag of the net.

well as a percentage of the catch value and made about $10 a ton. Gasoline was still an unfamiliar substance to most people and in 1899 there was an explosion aboard that injured several of the crew. The accident occurred when the men were injecting gasoline into seams and cracks in the hull to combat an infestation of bedbugs.

The ALPHA had two purse seines, one for sardines and the other for mackerel, patterned after an East Coast model. The sardine seine was 120 fathoms long and 8 fathoms deep with a one-inch mesh. The mackerel seine was 135 fathoms long by 17 fathoms deep and two-inch mesh. She could carry 16 tons of fish on deck, but the usual cannery limit was three or four tons per day The area fished was Santa Monica Bay, San Pedro Bay and around Catalina Island, but when they began targeting so-called "whitefish," such as yellowtail, barracuda and white seabass, they frequently fished at Catalina. That area was closed to commercial netting in 1917.

Brailing the catch into the deck bin.

Between 1895 and 1898 two other seiners were built in San Pedro and the three fished primarily for the canneries for the next 20 years. About 1912 the Mediterranean lampara round haul net was introduced for catching live bait and proved to be equally efficient for sardine fishing. It could be hauled entirely by hand from smaller boats, so the purse seiners began concentrating on "whitefish" such as barracuda, yellowtail and white seabass.

Catching tuna in lampara nets was not possible, but in 1915 bluefin tuna were taken with purse seines and the fishery boomed as new, larger, more efficient modern boats were built. By 1920 there were 125 purse seiners working out of San Pedro. At the present time nearly all the world's catch of tuna is taken with huge purse seines set by enormous ships ten times the size of the old ALPHA.

ALPHA's deckload of sardines.

Typical purse seiner in 1929.

SPORTFISHER II was built as a sportfishing boat, but converted to tuna fishing during World War II.

Commercial boat SAN ANTONIO was converted to sportfishing at San Diego in early 1930s.

ENDEAVOR was a purse seiner of the 1940-50s.

Left: MARIA ROSANNA is a modern steel tuna seiner.

The Redondo fishing barge THOMAS P. EMIGH was a casualty of the gale of April 5, 1932. (Courtesy Pierre Odier).

SUNSHINE II rode out the storm in the narrow lee of Santa Barbara Island.

Chapter 6
MISCELLANEOUS CATCH

The Awesome Gale of 1932

In the heyday of barge fishing sport craft were anchored or moored in the open sea at several locations along the South Coast. In the spring of 1932 unsettled weather for several days climaxed on April 20, in a 65 mph gale that wrought havoc with boats and barges exposed to the fury of the storm.

In the Redondo area three barges were driven ashore to become total wrecks. The barge MELROSE, an exferry, crashed into the rocks at White Point after vain, attempts to tow her to safety. As raging surf pounded the vessel a breeches buoy rescue of the five-man crew failed and the men made it to shore in a skiff only after the sea subsided.

The former three-masted steel bark GRATIA dragged onto the beach near Rocky Point and the THOMAS P. EMIGH, one time four-masted barkentine, stranded just south of the Monstad Pier. Both became total losses.

At Laguna Beach the former schooner CHARLES BROWN was wrecked and the ex-barkentine GEORGINA barely escaped destruction off Hermosa. RAINBOW off Long Beach was severely battered before her crew managed to drop a second anchor. In addition to the wrecked barges, many smaller fishing craft along the coast were victims of what was said to be the worst storm in 15 years. Similar disasters are now rare as there are no fishing barges moored offshore and smaller craft operate from sheltered ports.

The Great Storm of '39

After days of oppressive 100 degree heat, a furious tropical storm slammed into Southern California on 24 September 1939 with near hurricane-force winds and a deluge of rain. In those days, there were no satellites or ocean weather buoys to provide advance warning of the approaching gale. Fishing craft and weekend yachters were caught in the Catalina channel with tragic results.

The worst disaster ever to befall a sportfishing boat occurred when the SPRAY, returning from Anacapa Island, attempted to go alongside the pier at Point Mugu. As she turned toward the landing, a huge wave caught her in the trough and rolled her over. Her deckhouse was swept from the hull and 26 of the 28 souls aboard perished in the pounding surf. Horrified onlookers on the beach watched helplessly as the heads bobbing in the breakers disappeared one by one. Two battered survivors made it to the beach.

Capt. Billy Rice and 30 anglers on his famous SUNSHINE II spent an anxious night anchored in the narrow shelter of Santa Barbara Island. In Santa Monica Bay, Capt. Olaf Olsen's barge MINNIE A. CAINE parted

DISPATCH broke down and was towed by INDI-ANA and later cast adrift. The Coast Guard had to rescue her people.

her anchor chains and crashed ashore, and seven boats sank at their moorings. At Malibu, 54 patrons of the barge VIRGINIA A. were marooned aboard overnight, and the barge HIPPOGRIF foundered.

Sportboats INDIANA and DISPATCH were unable to debark their 60 passengers. Struggling toward San Pedro, DISPATCH broke down and was taken in tow by INDIANA, but was later cast adrift as too hazardous a burden. After a harrowing night, Coast Guard cutters rescued the people. Several boats were smashed against the San Pedro breakwater, and one boat was tossed clear over the rocks on a gigantic wave. Thirty boats were beached at Santa Barbara, and three vessels were lost while attempting to enter Newport Harbor, including the 140-foot yacht PARAGON, which had her side ripped out on the jetty rocks. At San Diego, a tuna clipper returning from the banks had to present her high bow to towering waves generated by 30-foot groundswells and back into the bay. All the piers along the coast were more or less severely damaged.

The Coast Guard had all seaworthy cutters out, and four Navy destroyers were also underway to aid those in distress. Few small craft in those days had radios, and in

INDIANA had to unload her passengers at San Pedro.

the aftermath of the gale over 50 boats were reported missing. Many rode out the storm in the lee of islands. It took several days for the Coast Guard to account for the dead and missing, and the final toll, in addition to the 26 lost on the SPRAY, was set at 18 from 12 vessels sunk or missing.

El Ninos Past and Present

By October of 1997 there was little doubt that the "Mother of all El Ninos" was underway, promising at least one more season of fabulous fishing. The downside of the situation was the likelihood of a wet and stormy winter with widespread damage, as seen in 1982-83, from high surf, flooding and mud slides. The '82-'83 El Nino was the strongest and most devastating ever, perhaps the worst in recorded history. The current gigantic surge of hot equatorial water began earlier than the others and is still building. Weathermen predicted a much more powerful El Nino than back in '82-83. The phenomenon can cause harmful changes in the world's weather patterns, resulting in shifts in the jet stream, monsoons and storm tracks.

The author with dorado taken during 1957 El Nino.

Arrival of the abnormally warm water from the central Pacific around Christmas time led fishermen in South America to coin the name "Christ Child," or "El Nino" in Spanish, for the event. El Nino can be disastrous to the vast anchovy fishery nourished by the cold Humboldt Current running along the South American shore. The tropical surges also push north from the Equator, driving ribbons of heated water far up the West Coast. These currents carry with them the pelagic game fish so highly regarded by saltwater anglers. The wandering fish typically travel far beyond their customary habitats.

Not much attention was paid to the El Nino phenomenon before the 1957-58 event. High sea temperatures

First marlin caught off Washington state in 1997.

and fish migrations have always been cyclical and taken as a matter of course. In March 1983 the National Marine Fisheries Service released information that there were El Ninos in 1891, 1925, 1931, 1941 and 1957-58. Historically, the strongest events have occurred in 1957-58, '65-'66, '72, '82-'83, '86-'87, '91-'92, and '94-'95. Some of these events had only minor effects on local weather and fishing. It is also possible that the great storms anticipated for the coming winter will not arrive. Weather, as often as not, fails to follow predicted patterns.

Warm water anomalies have occurred since before accurate records were kept. It seems that some episodes were so typical of the El Nino pattern that it is fairly certain that they were the real thing. There have also been warm-water seasons unrelated to equatorial surges. In 1936, conditions were favorable enough to bring schools of yellowfin tuna and skipjack to anchored boats at the Coronado Islands. Dorado and yellowfin were also present in great numbers off San Diego the following year.

Sport fishermen fondly remember '82-'83 for the unusually good fishing. In the San Diego area there was an influx of pelagic red crabs, millions of tiny crawdad-like critters drifting up on the warm flow. They showed up in May and in June acres of water around the Coronado Islands turned red with their swarming presence. Everything eats them and the flesh of some fish takes on a reddish hue when feeding on the crabs. They made excellent bait for all bottom fish and bass. I recall, for example, that the catch of humble sheephead and lowly rubberlip perch increased dramatically when the crabs were used for bait.

The effects of the giant El Nino were long-lasting and oceanographers measured a consequent wave of warm water in 1994, 12 years later. A sort of pulse of lesser El Ninos has followed the big one, appearing every two or three years. They have kept average sea temperatures above normal. Yellowfin tuna and skip-

jack, which prefer warm water, have been present off the South Coast each summer.

In 1997, elevated sea water temperature resulted in some of the best fishing of the century, especially for yellowtail. Record catches were posted all along the South Coast, with numbers growing by the day. It seemed likely that the total would add up to the largest yellowtail harvest ever, surpassing the 457,000 of the holdover year 1959.

"I never expect to see another year like this one," declared George Humphreys, owner of the three-quarter day boat MALAHINI, out of San Diego. By the last week of September, more than 10,000 yellowtail had been taken from his vessel. Humphreys stated that his boat had not caught even 1,000 yellows in a season, during the previous seven years.

One reason for the huge run-up in numbers is the small size of many of the fish, little four to six pound "Smedleys." The little guys have the same moxie and fighting heart as larger yellowtail, but are scarcely tackle-busters. Often biting with abandon, they ambitiously attack huge "bohunk" sardines nearly a foot long. Ideal targets for half-day fishing and rent rods, the small

Deckhand holds one of my "Smedleys."

69

The old man had a workout when he took ten of these yellowfin tuna on Tim Volklander's DOLPHIN.

yellows give many beginning anglers their first thrilling chance to battle one of the South Coast's prime game fish. The juvenile "'forktails" must be the offspring of last year's optimum spawning environment in Mexican waters. We can only hope the biomass is not endangered by the excessive number of subadult fish captured before they, in turn, have spawned.

The huge harvest of undersized yellowtail has prompted the California Department of Fish & Game to propose a new size limit for half of the 10-fish daily bag limit for sport-caught fish. Suggested is a minimum of 24 inches, measured from the fork of the tail, for five of the 10 allowed. A 28-inch limit is already in effect for commercials.

Not only have more forkies been taken to this date than ever before, but they have ventured far outside their usual territory. For the first time ever, a pair of yellowtail was captured at Kodiak, Alaska, over 2,000 miles north of their normal range, and there have even been reports of hookups by surf fishermen at Torrance Beach!

All sorts of marine animals follow warm currents up the coast. Fish & Game records for 1957-59 show no less than 50 different species of fish were found north of

their habitual locations. Bluefin, yellowfin and bigeye tuna were taken off Washington, barracuda were found in Canadian waters, white seabass in Alaska, bonito and skipjack swam off Oregon, and dorado cruised off San Francisco. The pattern repeated and it seemed likely the following two years would set new records for relocated fish.

The abundance of dorado off the South Coast is my best memory of the 1957-58 El Nino. I remember casting a jig at a paddy a mere three miles off the shore and the slamming strike of a 20-pounder that lurked there. There was also the time when I was piloting a Navy recreation boat and, after a fruitless offshore search for albacore, found a huge paddy only six miles from Point Loma. It held what must have been at least several hundred "dodos." Every bait that hit the water was instantly seized. It was "bendo" all around and leaping dolphin fish were visible on all sides of the boat, with lines dipping over and under in a mad Maypole dance. We left them after an hour, with over 70 dorado for 10 rods.

There was a holdover from that El Nino that provided super sport in 1959. Probably due to optimum spawning in the previous two years of warm seas, an all-time catch high was set for yellowtail. In addition, 1.2 million barracuda and 2,300 marlin were boated. If similar conditions prevail this time, it is likely that we will enjoy two more seasons of great fishing.

It is interesting to speculate on what part past El Ninos played in the apparent major shift of fish populations out of their present range. In the 1870s and '80s, the Monterey Spanish Mackerel (*Scomberomorus concolor*) was an important commercial fish abundant each fall in Monterey Bay. It closely resembles a Sierra mackerel, but without the golden spots. Around 1890, they disappeared. Forty years passed before a few lone specimens were caught in bait nets. A race of the mystery fish was later discovered in the upper reaches of the Sea of Cortez, a decidedly different environment from Northern California.

Until the 1890s, the center of the white seabass fishery was San Francisco. At the turn of the century there was a rapid shift of the seabass population to Southern California. At the very least, it appears that for a number of years the sea temperatures in the North were higher, and may have been the result of an El Nino.

We have seen a larger percentage of sardines, which thrive in warm water, appearing in our bait tanks. Northern anchovies, preferring cool water, are scarcer. A wholesale die-off of kelp beds has also occurred. Nutrient-rich cold water is required by the plants for healthy growth. Remember the huge beds at South Kelp and Middle Grounds at the Coronado Islands? They are long gone and the Point Loma and La Jolla beds show only a fraction of their former acres of dense growth. Kelp beds are vital to the ecosystem and destruction of the plants is sure to affect the species depending on them for food and shelter.

Another negative aspect of the hot sea is to suppress the cold upwellings that provide the nutrients supporting huge coastal fish populations. In June, the temperatures were as much as 14 degrees above normal along the central California coast. National Marine Fisheries Service scientists are very concerned about the effects on the growth and reproduction of resident species such as rockfish. John Hunter of NOAA's coastal fisheries division in La Jolla says, "Any cold water bottom fish is in for a rough reproductive season if the El Nino persists into the winter and spring of 1998. Bottom fish do not go with the flow as do many of the pelagic fish."

Salmon fishermen are also in dread of a possible drastic decline in their catch, such as that occurring in 1983. The dire climatic effects of an El Nino will not be addressed here; this discussion concentrates on fisheries.

On the upside, Dr. Alec McCall of NMFS notes that halibut tend to come on strong after a warming episode. "California halibut tend to peak consistently several years after an El Nino," he says.

Another benefit was the arrival off the South Coast in May, a full month early, of the highly esteemed and long-absent albacore. They also appeared off Half Moon Bay in the same month. They did not linger too long in the South, but provided prime sport before they swam away from uncomfortably warm water. San Diego sportboats managed to deck an impressive 36,429 longfin tuna before they vanished. Excellent albacore fishing continued in the Northwest throughout the summer.

According to the Dept. of Fish & Game, the excitement has also led to a 20 percent increase in the sale of angling licenses. Tackle merchants also reported a boom in business.

More surprises are no doubt in store as this season draws to a close. (I am anticipating the first catch of a wahoo on a San Diego day-and-a-half boat). Sensational fishing could well endure through the winter, but the expected monster storms may put an end to our angling paradise. We can, in any case, be grateful for a season the likes of which may not occur again in our lifetime. Stories of the great 1997 fishing year will pass into legend and be told and retold to a future generation of anglers.

Through late October 1997 dock totals for the San Diego sportfishing fleet were tabulated by Paul Morris at Fisherman's Landing as follows:

86,867 Yellowtail
38,336 Yellowfin tuna
26,329 Albacore
19,043 Dorado
4,970 Bluefin tuna
135 Bigeye tuna

As a result of the El Nino, larval bonefish and shortfin corvina were carried northward on warm currents and reintroduced into San Diego and Mission Bays and have furnished marvelous sport for light tackle anglers for ten years. Sadly, by 2010 these populations appear to be dwindling.

Harlan Major.

Harlan Major

For one who came late to ocean fishing, Harlan Major had a decided influence on the sport. His bestselling 1939 book *Salt Water Fishing Tackle* went through several editions and is a collector's item and one of my prized possessions. It still is a prime reference for prewar tackle research. His connection to South Coast fishing began when a friend, a member of the Tuna Club, introduced him to local and Catalina fishing. Major embraced the new hobby with enthusiasm and was quick to learn the necessary angling skills. During the 1920s, after several failed business ventures, he found himself a job as master of the fishing barge BLUE SEA off San Pedro. The vessel was a former decontamination and fumigation barge for the U.S. Public Health Service.

On 11 December, 1928 a savage storm overwhelmed the barge washing the deckhouse from the

Major (right) retrieved bodies from the sunken barge BLUE SEA and clung to submerged wreckage until rescued.

hull. Major and his crew of three clung to the mostly submerged wreckage as it drifted through churning seas. Two crewmen succumbed to hypothermia and died. Major, despite a broken elbow, lashed their bodies to the flotsam and stood knee deep throughout the night clinging to a rope for support. After 14 hours and at the limit of exhaustion the survivors were spotted by lookouts on the naval auxiliary USS PROCYON returning from fleet exercises.

With some daring work by a Navy boat crew the stoic Major and his men were rescued and taken to a hospital ship. After this remarkable feat of courage and endurance he founded a tackle and rod-making business and became a fishing writer of note. In 1937 Pan American Airways sent him on a survey of fishing possibilities at the proposed bases for Pacific overseas flights. In 1952 he wrote a second book, *Fishing Behind the Eight Ball,* about his adventures.

On the outbreak of the Second World War Major threw himself into organizing a project for collecting, overhauling and shipping fishing tackle to troops wherever there was fishable water. The gear was a great morale booster as, apart from relatively short intervals of action, most military time is spent in boring routine tasks.

I envy those who benefited from the gifts of tackle and surely could have used some myself during my time in the Solomon and Marshall Islands. Unfortunately, I never heard of the program until its termination after the war.

USS *PROCYON* sailors rescued Major and his mate.

Right: Versal skippered the SCOTTY and later owned her.

Versal Schuler 1953.

Remembering Versal Schuler

My first memory of Versal Schuler is from the mid-1930s when he piloted the SCOTTY, tender to the big barge STAR OF SCOTLAND. Although a young man at the time, he had already gained a reputation as a pleasant, quiet, reliable and hard working operator.

After beginning as a commercial fisherman set-lining for halibut, he graduated to operating sportfishing vessels. Never lacking for employment, he skippered a series of boats and worked as bait catcher for Santa Monica, Malibu and Ocean Park. After a stint in the Navy during World War II, he bought the INDIANA and operated her for a time from Malibu Pier.

In 1951, Schuler became partners with Fred Mullineaux as owner of the Ocean Park Pier sportfishing concession, and eventually bought out Fred's interest. In 1957, Schuler acquired the Santa Monica franchise from Bob Lamia and relocated to that landing. There he flourished, winning over the years a host of friends

BRIGHT I, Captain Homer "Deacon" Reinschmidt

INDIANA, Captain Orrin Winfield.

and dedicated customers for his boats.

Oldtimers will remember some of the craft pictured here. The great El Nino-generated storms of 1983 overwhelmed the wimpy breakwater at Santa Monica and completely demolished the pier and its boat landing. Schuler's business was destroyed, a crushing loss not only to him, but to the City of Santa Monica and to thousands of fishing patrons. Versal passed away in April of 1998, but fond memories remain of that honest, respected man and the fishing fun he provided for a legion of anglers.

KIAORA operated from Long Beach many years before moving to Santa Monica.

LOUISE ran from San Clemente Pier in 1946.

San Clemente Fishing

Located some six miles south of Dana Point, the SanClemente pier was the port for a series of sportfishing boats from the late 1920s until the Dana Point harbor was built nearby. A Captain Bert Jones first had boats INO, GLORIA, BERTHA, KOMOI and SIRIO, MARY LOU, ex-MARION G. DOUGLAS, a three masted schooner, was the barge affiliated with the enterprise.

In 1930 Scotty Lacade and John Creighton acquired the lease and moved their boats from overcrowded Santa Monica Pier. OWL, KITTIE A., VIRGINIA and GIULIO CESARE made up their fleet.

In 1935 the barge GEORGE U. HIND was there before being sold for service at Oceanside.

The business did fairly well, but was closed during World War II and did not reopen until April 1946 under the management of Woodrow Payne and John Norek. Boats were LOUISE and SILVER SPRAY.

Reflecting the good fishing to be had nearby and the popularity of the site, the business prospered and the fleet gradually grew to include six party boats, a barge and a bait boat. Photos show a few of the boats operating from the pier in the heyday of San Clemente sportfishing.

The Lacade-Creighton boats c. 1930.

SAN MATEO, Captain John Norek, was one of the newer postwar boats operating from San Clemente Pier.

73

NEPTUNE approaching the landing.

Old Hermosa

There was a time when every pier along the South Coast was the base for some kind of sportfishing operation. Most of the piers have long since vanished, destroyed by storms, fire or dismantling. Sport boats now run from sheltered harbors. Hermosa Beach Pier was no exception and opened for boat fishing in 1926 when Capt. J.M. Andersen and his partners built a landing stage to service the fishing barge OLYMPIC. Andersen's partner George Lewis' launch LILLIAN L. was the barge tender. The barge KOHALA was added in 1927, but sold a year later. In 1934 the OLYMPIC was retired and replaced with OLYMPIC II, which Andersen later moved to the Horseshoe Kelp. In dense fog on September 4, 1940 the barge was rammed by the Japanese steamer SAKITO MARU and sunk with a loss of eight lives.

From 1930-33 the Buebeck family ran mobile sportfishers from the Hermosa pier. They were MARTHA, CALYPSO, BIG REDONDO and LITTLE REDONDO. From 1934 to '36 Cliff Garner had the concession with boats GRANT, CALHEETA and ASAHI. Bait boat was Paul Froude's O & K. From 1936-38 the Bandini family had a former gambling ship as the fishing barge MAGDALENA BAY operating from the pier.

In 1937 Paul Froude obtained the concession and was in business until the war broke out in 1941. His fleet consisted of IRENE F., NEPTUNE, KINGFISH, ASAHI, GRANT and CALHEETA.

Paul Froude's business card.

After the war there was an effort to revive boat operations from the pier by Gary O'Neil with the boat PIER FISHER. He was succeeded by Mickey Pitman with the OFFSHORE, but both attempts were short-lived and no boats or barges have since been based at Hermosa. The photos displayed, from the Hollingsworth Collection give a glimpse of scenes at Old Hermosa.

Froude's IRENE F. Below: Cliff Garner's GRANT.

The barge OLYMPIC was served from Hermosa Pier.

Famous Farnsworth

During the early years of the 20th century, Catalina's heyday as the big-game sportfishing Mecca, "Tuna George" Farnsworth was the most sought after guide at the Avalon boat stands. His reputation for finding and catching fish was worldwide. His customers hauled in fabulous catches when others failed.

His father, an engineer working on roads, brought 17 year-old George to the island in 1900 and in a few short years the youth was established as a guide and boatman. Something of a loner, he kept his own counsel and studied the ways of the gamefish that swam in local waters. A keen observer, he wrote a daily log of conditions and catches. He developed such fishing instinct and skill that he could predict arrival time and locations of migrating schools of the big bluefin tuna that were the prime object of anglers' pursuit.

Farnsworth is best remembered as the inventor of kite fishing, a method of skipping a flying-fish bait across the head of a tuna school in a lifelike manner. With its use he was able to outfish all other guides and bring in big scores when they got nothing. He tried to keep the technique secret and resorted to all sorts of ruses to discourage competitors from following him to observe his methods. We would today

On August 22, 1913, William Boschen, inventor of the internal reel drag, caught the first broadbill on rod and reel. Guide George Farnsworth poses with one of his kites.

consider his secretiveness somewhat selfish, but it made him famous and he was able to pick and choose his customers. Many record catches were made with his guidance.

He hung on at Catalina long after many of his early patrons died or disappeared along with the big tuna. During World War II one of his angler patrons sold him his boat for $10 and in it he joined the commercial albacore fleet, jigging longfins for the canneries. In 1952, while far at sea, he suffered a massive stroke and spent the next seven years in and out of hospitals, finally passing away in 1959. His name is perpetuated by the fishing spot he discovered on the weather side of Catalina Island: Farnsworth Bank.

Farnsworth guided James Jump for his record 145 pound tuna on 27 pound test linen line in 1919.

The runaway trailer scooped up a dead palm tree.

Runaway Trailer

In April 1940, to get an early start on our season, my fishing friend Jack McDowd and I decided it would be a shrewd move to intercept the annual northward migration of barracuda schools. We would launch his 18-foot skiff at Newport Beach and follow the fish up the coast to Santa Monica Bay.

Jack's aunt had a beach house and would allow us to sleep in the garage for the duration of our stay in Newport. Jack rented a four-wheel flatbed trailer from Tedford's Boat Yard in Santa Monica, and we managed to block-up and load the heavy wooden boat from its winter storage site in his Hollywood back yard. The skiff was large for its type, with an inboard engine and a platform on the stem where a fisherman could stand while "wiggle-poling" for barries.

Next morning we made the haul to Newport with Jack's 1929 Model A Ford coupe and launched the boat in the bay. Our next chore was to return the trailer to Tedford. The trailer tongue was secured to the rear bumper with a length of light chain and we set off up the Pacific Coast Highway—old 101.

Barreling along at about 40 miles per hour, a goodly speed in the decrepit auto, we were passing through Huntington Beach when an astonishing sight caught my eye. Tearing along beside us was the unhitched trailer, making even greater speed than the car. Suddenly veering to the right, the trailer jumped the curb, narrowly missing a bus-stop bench, and smashed into a fat palm tree.

Flying into the air, the severed tree trunk landed on the trailer's bed as neatly as if it was intended to ride there. It was our great good fortune that there was no one waiting at the bus stop, nor any cars or buildings near enough to be damaged by the runaway trailer. A hit from it would have been lethal.

Shaken and apprehensive that we might run afoul of the law, we backed up the Ford and reattached the trailer, this time with more care and additional passes of chain through the eye of the tongue. The tree was too heavy to lift, so we left it where it was. Tedford must have been mystified to find it on the trailer, which we dropped off at the yard after dark. We were already back in Newport when he came to work next morning.

The expected great run of barracuda fizzled, and after a couple of weeks of scratch fishing, Jack cruised his boat back to Santa Monica. I liked the ambience of Newport, which at the time was a major fishing port, and found employment at King's Landing as a deckhand on the sport-boats VALENCIA III and SUNSHINE. There I remained until October when gathering war clouds activated my entry into the Navy.

Ad for planned long-range trips.

Long Ranger Wreck

Frank Kiessig pioneered long range fishing trips in 1936 when he sent his SPORTFISHER II to Cabo San Lucas and Guadalupe Island. During World War II sport fishing boats were prohibited from operating out of San Diego. When the ban was lifted in 1946 Otto Kiessig, son of the innovative owner, built three new vessels. Two were steel-hulled 65-footers designed with long range fishing in mind. A 42-footer was for local fishing.

On the night of January 5, 1947 the new SPORTFISHER V, skippered by her owner Otto Kiessig, was cruising south along the Mexican coast on a scheduled

The new SPORTFISHER V.

SPORTFISHER V wrecked on Geronimo Island.

10-day trip. Around 10 P.M. in rough seas and foggy weather she suddenly crashed into a reef near Geronimo Island, 190 miles from San Diego. Four of the 18 people aboard, hurled to the deck or into machinery by the sudden impact, were injured. The cook was washed overboard and lost, the only fatality. Those in their bunks were unharmed.

After a night long ordeal of tossing from reef to reef in pounding surf, the sinking boat stranded and survivors were helped ashore by inhabitants of the island. Aboard was a doctor who provided emergency treatment for the injured. The boat's radio had already summoned aid and the passing tuna clipper JOAN OF ARC came to the rescue. With her motorboat she took aboard the shipwreck victims and transferred the injured to a Coast Guard plane on the morning of the seventh. The others were returned to San Diego on the tuna boat. The SPORTFISHER V was a total loss.

It was a wreck that should never have happened. The notorious Sacramento Reef adjacent to the island was well known to mariners as a hazard to be given a wide berth. Small craft radars were not yet available, but careful navigation, course plotting and alert watch keeping would have kept the boat well offshore from the dangerous Mexican coast. Hundreds of commercial fish boats and merchant craft were continuously sailing coastwise without mishap. It is noteworthy that such accidents are very rare in modern times, but the lessons were well learned. Superbly equipped boats and strict Coast Guard regulations for crews are responsible for an outstanding safety record by today's long rangers.

Otto Kiessig (left) with a typical long range catch.

Tuna clipper JOAN OF ARC rescued survivors.

Frank Kiessig's original SPORTFISHER.

Coincidence

In the fall of 2005 old-timer George Cowen was waiting for the chair in the shop of his longtime barber and found one of my books among the reading materials available for customers. As he read my tales of fishing as it was in the long ago, he realized that he and I had shared many common experiences. George looked up my number in the phone book and called me with an invitation to go bay fishing in his dandy, well-equipped boat. And so our friendship began.

During our fishing trips together we chatted about our teenage fishing obsessions and the wonderful catches we enjoyed at the Coronado Islands in the old days. I learned that he had been a regular on Frank Kiessig's SPORTFISHER during the 1930s.

It so happened that my first excursion on a San Diego sportboat at age 16 was aboard SPORTFISHER on August 23, 1935. I had joined a group of Santa Monica anglers who made the journey south in the panel truck of a character known as "Tin Bucket" as he customarily carried his handline and other tackle in a pail. On this trip he brought a rod and reel. We passengers each paid 50 cents for the gasoline consumed.

George Cowan, aged 15, caught these yellowtail and bluefin tuna at the Coronado Islands in 1935 from Frank Kiessig's original SPORTFISHER.

The fishing at North Coronado was good and I was thrilled when I managed to boat five yellowtail, one of 23 pounds, a jackpot contender until bluefin tuna showed up. The deckhand chumming atop the bait tank was handing out choice sardines to a young lad about my age who was obviously a skilled fisherman and was doing very well. Every time he would hook up the head deckhand. Tex Miller, would holler, "Georgie has another one!" He and other crewmen took special care to assist the boy in clearing tangles and following his fish.

I was somewhat envious of the special attention the lad received and surmised that he was a son or other close relative of the boat's owner. I thought to myself that if I got the same attention I would also be a highliner. I clearly recalled that trip, that special young man, and the favoritism of the crew. As George and I fished the bay and reminisced, I asked him if he perhaps was that lad I still remembered after all these years. It turned out he was that very person and explained that for some reason the boat's owner had taken a special liking for him and the crew was aware of it.

So, 70 years later we realized that even though we grew up in different cities and were not personally acquainted, we had fished on the same trip as 'teens and both cherished memories of the marvelous fishing a lifetime ago and the trip we shared. It really is a small world!

George was befriended by Frank Kiessig.

South Seas Success

It was nearly four decades ago that Rick Pollock, a young fishing fanatic, was deckhand for me when I skippered the charter boat EL LOBO, and was later himself her captain . Five years later, in November of 1978, he migrated to New Zealand to run a boat catering to overseas anglers, mainly from California. After obtaining permanent residency, he alternated between commercial and sport fishing for five years. In 1985 he purchased PURSUIT, a lobster boat, converted her for sport fishing and built a business with mostly local clients. With fishing savvy and hard work numerous national and world record caches were established and tournaments won. Live bait techniques learned in California were adapted and remain the hallmark of the operation. Better range and accommodations were needed for the expanding enterprise and a new 52-foot PURSUIT was built in 1997. Aside from the largest bait tank in NZ, full walk-around decks and creature comforts for the passengers are appreciated by customers and assure full bookings even with tough economic conditions. The fabulous sport fishing available in New Zealand was first brought to the notice of U.S. anglers by Zane Grey with a 1926 book enthusing over the abundance of marlin and giant yellowtail in the sea and rainbow trout in the rivers. Rick has sent me copies of his trip reports and photos of some of the humongous game fish taken from his boat. There are some monsters strange to our coast, but the albacore and yellowfin tunas are the same seasonal visitors to our waters. Apart from striped marlin, the most familiar would be the yellowtail, called kingfish in NZ. For whatever reason, the fish down there grow much larger.

There are several other varieties of good eating and hard fighting fish also to be had. Some are semitropical types that we would encounter only in Mexican seas, such as redsnappers and trevallys. There is also a huge

Rick stroking an albacore on EL LOBO, 1973.

bass that resembles our own giant, but with larger eyes.

If I was still physically capable of the travel and strenuous stand-up effort, I would love to make the journey to NZ and walk the deck and sample the thrill of fishing in strange seas with an old friend from long ago. As it is, I am happy with the vicarious thrill I get from reading Rick's newsletter accounts of adventures in the PURSUIT.

Captain Rick today.

Huge yellowtail caught in 2001.

Hapuku, a sort of bass, is a favorite in NZ.

79

Brown Water Fishing

A prime fishing area in Santa Monica Bay for sport and commercial boats in the 1920s and '30s was off Playa del Rey and El Segundo. Due to tidal flows and currents, many acres of sea water in that area were often colored a muddy brown by the discharge from the Hyperion sewer outfall. The first wastewater pumping plant and a pipeline pier were completed in 1894. Odd as it may seem, fishing was permitted from the pier and was carried on as late as 1925.

All of Los Angeles and environs dumped their sewage there and it bubbled to the surface in a huge boil containing tons of nasty flotsam. In spite of the pollution large schools of smelt gathered to feed off bits of garbage, or whatever, and they in turn attracted sea birds and gamefish such as barracuda and white seabass. Halibut fishing nearby was sometimes excellent also. I recall occasions when the brown water spread for miles, but was only a thin layer about a foot thick on the surface. Stirring with a gaff or oar would reveal the cleaner water under the dirty film. In May of 1947 I caught seabass trolling jigs right around the boil. Much to my surprise, a lone, lost salmon came my way in the brown water and a year later I got a nice eight-pound steelhead there. I also caught several discarded condoms.

A lot of barracuda fishing was done in the area and I last trolled there for some good scores using bone and aluminum jigs in the spring of 1949. Due to the population explosion in the county a new sewage plant opened in 1950 and subsequent expansions of treatment facilities have been built, including another seven-mile outfall.

Sadly, from reports I read it seems that fishing in the bay has deteriorated badly from what it was before the 1960s. One can only speculate as to whether or not the huge volume of wastewater discharged is the cause, but it is logical to suppose that it is at least partly to blame. It is my opinion that human-generated waste and industrial runoff are more responsible for generally poor catch results than overfishing.

I jigged a lot of barracuda in the brown water.

This dandy 17 lb. salmon was a surprise catch.

Left: Fishing on the Hyperion outfall pier in 1925.

Handlines

When I was a pup 80 years ago many folks still fished with handlines from the many piers and even from the mobile "live bait boats." A cheap ball of twisted cotton twine was available at any hardware or variety store. Fishing nets and commercial trolling and setlines were fashioned from it. I wound mine on a stick and carried it to and fro in a cloth flour sack that doubled as a container for the small fish I caught from Santa Monica Pier. Eventually I succeeded in capturing my first bonito, but prestigious halibut and barracuda eluded me and I yearned to sample them.

On my first trips aboard the half-day boat FAITH I had little success except with mackerel. I had only my crude sidewinder reel and short, jointed yellow cane rod and lacked the skill and knowhow to catch the desirable species. The proper way to attach a live anchovy to my hook had yet to be mastered I never got to fish from the choice stern positions which the adult regular customers occupied.

I wheedled my way on an afternoon trip aboard the Faith for 50 cents and we fished at the "101 Kelp," the first bed north of the pier, near Santa Monica Canyon. I was not doing well and managed only a small bass. It was extremely frustrating and I thought to double my chances I would also drop my handline and let it soak while using my primitive rod and reel.

I was fishing on the port side forward of the bait tank on the lightly loaded boat and secured the line to the chain lifeline that was supported by pipes fitted in holes in the low caprail. As the afternoon wore on I would periodically check the handline for possible biters. I lost several baits, but never felt any nibbles.

At last it was time to return to the pier and the skipper hollered, "Lines up!" At the last minute I began to retrieve the handline and lo, there was some resistance. To my intense delight and surprise there came to the surface a nice little halibut of about two pounds! I bounced the little flattie and excitedly announced to the bored deckhand that I had not felt anything on my line prior to pulling it. It was my very first halibut catch and thus the memory remains clear and happy in my mind to this day. I proudly presented the fish to my parents for a welcome and tasty dinner.

In those years of the Great Depression and subsistence fishing there was widespread use of handlines and jackpoles on sport fishing boats. Such tackle was usually tolerated except on San Diego boats and a few vessels fishing at Catalina. I continued using handlines off and on when it was appropriate and a large catch of fish was needed for sale. After World War II the use of handlines by passengers was eliminated except for a few special deep water rock cod trips.

FAITH, Morris half-day boat in 1932.

W.K. was Morris backup boat for charter, all-day or half-day trips.

W.K. photo shows typical layout of Morris boats. Bench seating and chain lifeline are visible

The Importance of Slime

It saddens me somewhat when I hear cocky deckhands and high-falutin' anglers disrespectfully refer to barracuda as "slime." They once were a very prominent part of the fishing picture on the South Coast. When I was a teenage "kid commercial" in the 1930s we usually called them snakes or scooters. The big ones were logs or stovepipes and little ones were shorts or pencils.

An event of significance was the reappearance every Spring of barracuda in Santa Monica Bay. Usually it occurred in April or May, but occasionally as early as February or March. The fish were extremely important to the sportfishing industry from Santa Barbara to Newport Beach and good catches drew thousands of anglers. So popular were they that newspapers headlined their arrival. The scooters were not hard to hook and could put a bend in a bamboo rod, but were not too difficult to handle even for unskilled beginners, kids and ladies. In a 1968 survey by the Dept. of Fish and Game a majority of landing operators named barracuda the most important species overall, with kelp bass, yellowtail and bonito next in order of rank.

During the truly desperate years of the Great Depression, when unemployment reached 25 percent, they were valued as an inexpensive source of protein. Gillnetting and trolling were the usual commercial fishing methods, with trolled or hook-caught fish preferred over netted fish as being less apt to be bruised and mushy. Barracuda were found in every retail fish market and restaurant year around. They were also the target of intense winter commercial fishing in Mexican waters. Because of their abundance they were relatively inexpensive to buy whole or chunked and were usually

These boys will try to peddle their catch.

baked, or steaked in one and a half or two inch slices and fried. They were also excellent when smoked. I recall that the Ralph's market in Santa Monica sold them for 10 cents a pound on a fairly regular basis, and sometimes on sale for less.

During all my teenage years I made all my own spending money catching and peddling fish. Aside from the fun of catching the fish, it entailed a lot of hard work and dawn to dark effort.

Folks would flock to the pier landing every afternoon when the boats came in to buy fresh fish at bargain prices from debarking anglers. I sold barries for as little as 10 cents apiece, and as much as 50 cents each when they were large or scarce. In the summer of 1935 Castagnola, the fish dealer in Santa Barbara, sent a refrigerated truck to Santa Monica to buy barracuda for 3 cents a pound for all you could catch. A dollar then was worth many times as much as it is today and we loved barracuda as good money makers.

A typical catch from the live bait boat SCANDIA II, c.1930.

Souvenirs From the Files

In the early post-World War II years sportfishing enjoyed a tremendous boom from renewed prosperity and pent-up demand. As I browse through my files from those days I find souvenirs I had nearly forgotten. Recently I came across my first attempts at writing for an outdoor magazine. A small series of articles called "Know Your Gamefish," illustrated with my pen and ink drawings, was published in the California Fish & Game News 64 years ago in 1947. The pub was a weekly edited by Ken Bayliss in Glendale and usually ran from 24 to 32 pages.

It was also a time of transition from old tackle and methods to new ways of catching fish. As a result of my articles the DuPont company sent me a flattering request for a story touting the advantages of using their new nylon monofilament on spinning reels. At the time I had never used a spinning reel and barely knew what they were. Popular in Europe, veterans serving there discovered them and brought samples back to the U.S. I had used monofilament only for surf fishing leaders and was impressed by its transparency and strength, but few anglers were using it as a main line on reels because the early production was somewhat stiff and brittle.

Nylon had been used for parachute shroud lines during the war and its strength and durability was proven. Experimental cords of twisted nylon were tried as a substitute for the fragile linen fishing lines in use for a century. At first they were not successful as their absolute limpness made them tangle too easily, but when braiding was tried they became instantly popular. Most of the early types were flat like ribbon and dyed green, but were a vast improvement, their resistance to rot being the greatest advantage over the old vegetable linens. It was no longer necessary to strip and dry after each use and a drop of blood or spot of rust was not fatal.

New materials for rods and reels were also being tried and eventually the light weight and superstrong fishing tools in use today superseded the old bamboo rods and heavy metal reels.

The fragile yellowed pages of the old pub offer up some interesting ads for the transitional tackle and gear in use at the time. Here are a few samples:

1947 ad for nylon monofilament.

Supposed to deter line grooving.

Wire leaders were still favored.

Fileted sardines in a jar.

This twisted line was too soft.

This painting was made for my friend, and host to commemorate my trip of a lifetime.

The Trip of a Lifetime

Bring your passport up to date. The boat is in Panama and we will fly down and fish our way to Costa Rica," was the phone message I got from my friend and patron Bob Fulton in February of 1994. Bob was my favorite charter customer when I skippered the six-pack FOGGY during the late 1970s. It was my great good fortune to have made such a friend. A self-made millionaire civil engineer, he was the most congenial, generous, down-to-earth customer I ever encountered. He and members of his family made frequent trips with me for all kinds of San Diego fishing: offshore, Coronado Islands, Mexican coast and local. We had a very cordial relationship. When the FOGGY's owner passed on the heirs sold her and I was temporarily out of a skippering job.

"Who are we going to fish with now?" asked Bob. I suggested Oscar Olsen, owner of the WINDSONG. For several years Bob and his family, friends and employees fished with Oscar and I was always invited to come along as a guest. We enjoyed many memorable

trips. Bob eventually bought a large Florida sportfishing yacht and spent some time fishing Florida and Caribbean waters. I hadn't seen him for a couple of years so it was a great thrill for me to receive his call and invitation. As an old Navy guy, I use the 24-hour clock. Here is the log I kept:

Tuesday 15 Feb. 1994
0730 Depart San Diego for Dallas
Arrived Panama 2030. Wild taxi ride to Balboa Yacht Club where boat is anchored out. Picked up in the dinghy. Soon sacked out.

AUDACIOUS is a Lydia design, 70 feet overall length, built at Stewart, Florida in 1969. Double planked mahogany hull sheathed with fiberglass. Twin 840 hp V-10 Mann diesels and two 20 kw Northern Lights generators. Interior air conditioning.

Captain: Richard Hoffman, Mate: Steve Fowler. Anglers: Bob Fulton, owner, and guest Ed Ries.

Wednesday 16 Feb. 1994
Waiting for clearance all morning.

1700: Underway from Balboa Yacht Club, Panama. Passing through the roadstead we see ships of all nations anchored, awaiting their turn to transit the Canal. Proceeding at 20 knots all night. I took the wheel watch 2100 to 2400. Many radar targets. Position determined by SatNav system.

Thursday, 17 February.
0730. Off Punta Mala. Water temperature is very warm: 85.5F. Began trolling at 10 knots. The bait-and-switch method is used. Two teasers streamed from each outrigger, designated "rigger" and "flat." Teasers are large Mold-Craft soft plastic lures without hooks. Flat teasers are controlled from the bridge and riggers from two custom short rods and reels mounted on the fishing chair. Ready rods with live bait attached are in tube holders. When fish rise to the teasers the lures are wound in, coaxing fish close to the boat. Live bait on a ready rod is then presented and the fish will usually seize it. After the hook up they are generally fought stand-up style unless the battle is drawn out and the fish is very large.

Line class rigs for sailfish: 4, 8, 16, 30 lb. test line. For marlin and big tuna: 50, 80 and 130 lb test.

Live baits are goggle-eye jacks, known in Mexico as caballitos, or other small fish. Baits are attached to 9/0 or 10/0 forged hooks snelled to heavy monofilament leaders 12 to 15 feet in length. Light tackle rigs have 200 lb test leaders and heavy rigs have 300 to 500 lb. All hooks are sharpened. Leaders are secured to lines with a special knot that will pass through rod guides. A small loop of Dacron or dental floss is passed through the nose of the bait with a special needle about 9 inches long. An opening in the side of the needle eye eases the

Bob Fulton, friend, patron and generous host.

procedure. A lark's head knot ties the loop back on the hook and the bait is stored head down in one of three special cylindrical wells in the after bulwarks. The immobilized bait will live for hours as the water flow in the tubes keeps them well aerated.

A catch is considered legitimate when the leader is brought to the mate's grasp, which is where the fish could be easily gaffed if desired. The mate pulls the fish up as far as possible and extracts the hook or cuts the leader as close as he can.

0830: I bait my first sailfish but she throws a hook after a few jumps.

1001-1021: I bring a nice sailfish, my first, to leader on 16 lb. mono. Many jumps. The sailfish "light up" when feeding by turning almost purple-black. It is a great thrill to watch them nail the bait.

1058: A marlin rises to a teaser, but fades away before it can be baited.

1150: Bob hooks a very active sailfish and brings it to leader in 10 minutes.

1430: After a great aerial display I capture my second sailfish, a real jumper, on 8 lb test in about 10 minutes. It was a surface fight, which makes it much easier to win with light tackle. Richard says it was a big fish, about 120 lbs.

AUDACIOUS in Panama.

1630: We approach Islas Jicaron and Jicarita and troll

Marauder jigs on surface and a planer. Black skipjack are a nuisance as we are hoping for wahoo or a large snapper. We get neither, but can't keep crevallys and skipjacks off the hooks. We also get a threadfin jack and I haul in an amberjack of about 20 lbs. Something huge breaks off the planer rig. I boat a large sierra for the last catch of the day.

1850: Anchored in seven fathoms in the lee of Isla Jicaron. Steve transforms the sierra into a marvelous ceviche dish.

Friday, 18 February
0845: Underway towards the famed Hannibal Bank, seven miles northwest of Jicaron.

1000: Bob brings a large sailfish almost to leader on 8 pound, but the line breaks.

1115: I blew it. Got two jumps from a nice sail before she threw the hook. Steve says I let her take it too long and she spit it before the hook was set.

1135: Raised a sail, but she left us after one pass at the bait.

1202-1330: I fought a large sailfish on 8 pound line. She dogged deep and jumped only once after a spectacular head-out, sail-up strike. More drag was applied in an effort to end the stubborn battle and the line finally parted. Suffering greatly from overheating during the long contest, I had to shower and get into my air-conditioned bunk for a rest.

1535: Up and ready for more. We are near Isla Montuosa in 7/20 north latitude. Reminds me of San Martin. Trolling plugs for wahoo. We get several large crevallys instead.

1804: Anchored northeast side of Montuosa. Tried to

Monstrous blue marlin.

catch some bait with Yo-zuri bait catcher rig, but got mostly grunts, which Richard says, are not very good bait. Did catch a pretty little creole fish and a small snapper.

Saturday, 19 February .
0830: Underway with teasers out. Current got across the breeze and we spent a somewhat bumpy, wakeful night.

0903: Bob's line broken after a sailfish fell on it.

0910-0917: Bob brings a sail to leader on 16 lb.

1005: A sailfish intrigued by teaser, but would not eat bait.

1010: I hooked a sail that made two jumps and sounded. Came unbuttoned after 40 minutes.

1100-1112: Bob hooks and brings to leader an estimated 275 lb. black marlin. A nice acrobatic fish.

1255: Hot and glassy calm,. I bring a sail to leader on 16 lb. line in about four minutes. Amazing! She never jumped. Two fish were raised and the first one threw the bait after a couple jumps. As I reel in the mangled bait, the second fish truck and she was the one I caught.

1630: Bottom fishing for edibles in 70-75 fathoms with electric reel and wire line. Rig is similar to a downrigger set up. Five-hook gangion baited with cut skipjack. Three groupers and numerous unidentified rockfish or sculpin types, also some whitefish, were taken.

1735: Anchored at Montuosa. I sketched a mystery fish for later ID. Delicious blackened filet of grouper for supper. I catch a beautiful perch-like fish on the bait rig. Side streaked with bright blue, yellow fins and tail. Fed our bait with grouper scraps. Creole fish was

Blue marlin stirring up a great patch of foam.

Steve wets me down with the deck hose

very aggressive and nipped my finger.

Sunday, 20 February.
0825-0834: After a few jumps, I lose a sailfish on 4-pound.

1004-1031: Bob plays and loses a sailfish on 4-pound.

1200: Heading for Punta Barica. Blue water, no fish. Interrogating Richard, I gather he must have presided over least 5,000 billfish encounters in over 20 years of constant fishing. He makes a very accurate weight estimates and can spot fish under the teasers and below the surface like nobody I've ever seen. The Australian mate Steve learned his skills as a leader man in the black marlin fishery at Cairns. They're both real fishing professionals and I'm lucky to have such experts guiding me.

1220: Schools of skipjack are breaking on bait. They try to eat the swivels on the teaser lines and boobies are diving on the teasers. Looks very fishy here.

1233: A marlin rises to the teaser and I toss a blue runner bait to her on the 50 lb. rig. I hook up and get in the chair as the fish takes off. After a few leaps, she thrashes around stirring up a great patch of foam and then sounds and heads for China. I settle in for a prolonged fight and am lucky to have her on a two-speed Shimano Tiagra reel. Steve wets me down with the deck hose and plies me with cold drinks to keep my temperature down. After an hour of strenuous give-and-take it seems that I can bring her no closer. Richard says to loosen the drag and he will try to outmaneuver the beast. He speeds the boat in a circle and positions me in front of the fish so that I am pulling from dead ahead instead of over her shoulder. Apparently confused, the marlin is drawn closer by my frantic pumps and high-gear winding. At last we see color and she appears monstrous, unbelievably huge. A few more pumps and Steve gets the leader as Bob tries to snap photos. She flurries alongside as Steve cuts her loose close to the hook. I'm still in the chair, exhausted and gasping for breath. Declares Richard from the bridge: "Congratulations, Ed! It was a blue marlin and a big one, about 750 pounds." Steve says he thought her about 800! I am in heaven! The biggest thing I have ever had on a line in 65 years of fishing. At age 75 it was also a catch that tested the limits of my ability to cope with the physical stress involved.

1421-1440: Bob gets a sail on 16 lb.

1445: Bob baits a big tuna. Huge boil and spit the bait. Chasing porpoises and bird schools.

1536: Double tuna strikes on teasers, but no bites on bait.

1559-16 08: Bob gets a sail on 30 lb. line. We remain with porpoises all afternoon, frequently dropping back live bait, but no biters. Richard orders hooks in two teasers.

1701-1752: Smashing tuna strike on a purple and pink lure. Bob brings in a fish to gaff on the 80-pound rig.

Leadering Bob's yellowfin tuna.

87

Bob fights a sailfish as Steve looks on.

After careful measurements and applications of the formula, the weight is calculated at 242.27 lbs.

1910: Anchored in the lee of Islas Ladrones. Very dangerous looking rocks. Water is a hot 86 degrees. Tuna steaks for dinner.

Monday, 21 February.
0750: Underway. Richard says tuna-like fishes on their backs "go to sleep." Their metabolism slows and that is why they live so long in the cylindrical wells.

1015: No fish. In lines and run for Golfito. As we pas Punta Barica we leave Panamanian waters and the time zone changes to same as U.S. Central.

1240: Anchor at Golfito, Costa Rica. Launch Zodiac to fetch Port Captain.

1600: Move to Eagle's Nest Marina for refueling.

1815: Ashore to Rancho Grande, a Cafe, for a steak dinner.

Tuesday, 22 February.
1210: Richard returns with "zarpe" (cruising permit).

1250: Underway. Leave Golfo Dulce.

1410: Start trolling.

1500: I hook a sail on 16 lb. that puts on a great show of tail walking and jumping before Bob can handle the leader and release.

1645-1650: Bob makes an easy sailfish catch on 30 lb. line.

1835: Anchor at Isla Del Cano.

Wednesday, 23 February.
0720: Underway.

0855-0904: I catch a nice sailfish. Bob handles the leader. Fish got on swimstep while thrashing around.

0908: Bob as a hit and spit strike

0954: We approach a small commercial boat in response to frantic waving. No trouble-they just want to bum "cigarillos." We trade two packs for two amarillo snappers that we have for breakfast next day. I don't see how the little boat can support the seven fishermen aboard.

1430: Trolling amidst the Quepos sport fleet. We get three rises on teasers but no biters.

1600: Have seen at least 50 jumping sailfish, some very close to the boat, but they ignore our teasers. Strange.

1730: Anchor at Quepos, C.R.

Thursday, 24 February
0718: Underway.

0838-0843: Bob catches and releases a sail. Two fish

Captain Richard Hoffman fighting a cow tuna.

rose, but I was too slow getting another bait in.

0924-0933: I got a dandy sailfish on 16 lb. Stayed near the surface and jumped nicely close to the boat.

1144: I baited another sail, but she jumped off. She hit the other bait and spit it.

1147-1220: Three fish chased the teasers. None would bite. Jumpers are frequent.

1255: I baited and hooked a big tuna on 30 lb. rig. Line broke at 1345. Just as well--I never would've got her. For the first half hour she did not know she was hooked. She just kept swimming around with a school of porpoises and didn't come to life until the porps took off.

1400: Stop on tuna. Bob and I both miss strikes. My reel jammed.

1445: Richard, unable to stand the sight of puddling tuna, comes off the bridge and toss a bait for an instant hook up on 80-pound. Fighting the fish with stand-up gear until he gets color on an estimated 250-pounder.

1510: Fish dives under the boat and line hits swimstep. Pop! Harness prevents dipping rod tip in time. Damn! Too bad.

Our Aussie mate Steve Fowler with a black skip-jack.

ROUTE OF THE *AUDACIOUS*

1516: Bob and I get tuna of 25 and 30 lbs. Until 1800 we chased porpoise school, sliding and dropping baits back. Several strikes and I lost a big one on heavy tackle when the hook pulled out after 20 minutes. Bob got another about 50 lbs.

1700: In lines and run for the barn.

1840: Anchored in Bahia Ballena.

Friday 25 February
0653: Underway.

0810: Started trolling off Cabo Blanco.

0838-0843: I bait and catch a good sailfish on 16 lb line.

1105-1110: Bob captures a jumping fool of a sailfish.

11311-138: My last fish puts on a great acrobatic display and spits the hook and releases herself while Bob is holding the leader.

1230: In lines and run for Puntarenas.

1455: Anchor in Puntarenas, Costa Rica. We have a long taxi ride to the capital city, San Jose, to catch a flight home. End of a wonderful experience.

My score: one blue marlin, seven sailfish, one yellowfin tuna, one amberjack and several lesser species. It truly was my "Trip of a Lifetime" and will always be my most cherished fishing memory.

It was my last and best adventure with Bob Fulton. He passed away on 6 August 1995.

Bob Fulton fighting a big tuna.

Ed struggles with the blue marlin.

Bob's cow yellowfin tuna estimated at over 242 lbs.

Blue marlin flurry at leader, pectora fin in the air.

Ed with a close-in sailfish jumper.

The Turning Point

It has been 70 years since the U.S. entry into World War II. For many in my generation the war was the most significant event in our lives, and the turning point from which all prior and subsequent happenings are measured. As a result of the war, great changes took place in all aspects of life, and nowhere were they more pronounced than in the sport and business of ocean fishing.

For ten years prior to the war, the Great Depression deflated the economy and left millions homeless and unemployed. Subsistence fishing was commonplace and sport was often secondary. Peddling sport-caught fish was condoned by the state as long as the seller had a ten-dollar commercial license and abided by commercial size limits, such as three pounds for barracuda and four pounds for halibut. No limits on size or numbers were imposed for kelp and sand bass. They were prized market fish, ranking below only halibut and white seabass, and restaurants preferred the smaller ten to twelve inch bass. The overfished resource was saved by the size and possession limits established in 1954.

Commercial fish boats from San Diego pursued yellowtail, tuna and seabass at the Coronado Islands, using live sardines on handlines. Hundreds of small craft worked from piers and ports along the entire West Coast, gillnetting, trolling, trapping and setlining for whatever edible species were available. Fish canneries at Monterey, San Pedro, Newport Beach and San Diego put up huge packs of sardines, mackerel and tuna, providing needed employment for thousands.

Sportfishing boats were crude and slow by today's standards. The majority were converted commercial craft, and many were driven by dangerous gasoline engines. A timepiece and a compass were the sole navigational aids on most boats. There were few comforts for passengers. Galleys, bunks and radios were rare and began to appear only in the late 1930s, notably in San Diego. Some boats permitted jackpole and handline fishing, especially in the early years when rod-and-reel tackle was a luxury.

War industries and full employment resulted in a California population explosion that endures to this day. A huge, pent-up demand resulted in a tremendous expansion in fishing enterprises. Almost no items of tackle or equipment remained unchanged from prewar days. New materials for rods, reels, lines and lures resulted in more efficient tackle and bigger catches. Fast, built-for-the-purpose boats equipped with sophisticated electronics and hulls of aluminum, plywood, and fiberglass began replacing the tired, old prewar hulls.

Commercial fishing also boomed for about twenty years, but is now nearly defunct due to increasing restrictions and closures generated by the political clout of vast numbers of recreational anglers and the enviroterrorists who want to eliminate all fishing. Another turning point was passed when the canneries closed and the big tuna boats departed. All marketed seafood will soon be imported or farm-raised. It is no longer possible for a person to simply get a boat, a license, some hooks and lines and just go fishing for the market. Nobody wants to try fishing for a living in the present circumstances.

* * * * *

At age 92 I have reached another turning point in my life. I am no longer physically able to venture out on the sea that has been so much an influence and part of my life. I feel that the modern hi-tech world is fast leaving me behind. Keeping up with all the new and wonderful fishing tools and methods is becoming difficult. So be it. I have had a long and interesting run with adventures that can never again be duplicated. I am content to live with my memories. If my tales and reminiscences furnish a bit of insight into our fishing history, I will be pleased.

Farewell, fellow fishermen! May all your baits get bit and all your catches thrill. Catch a big one for me.

Author Ed Ries holds up one of the many fish caught in San Diego Bay.

PART II

MIKE McCORKLE, THE ECLECTIC FISHERMAN

Mike McCorkle was a pinhead (apprentice deckhand) for Captain Bruce Barnes on the STAR ANGLER, seen here fishing at the Horseshoe Kelp off San Pedro.

Mike with his first catch, a Mammoth Creek trout.

Mike still has the Spin-Cutta rod.

Chapter 7

FIRST NIBBLES AND FISHING JOBS

clectic adj: to pick, selecting from various systems, doctrines or sources.

In his fishing career Mike has certainly been more than average eclectic. His story begins: I was born Nov. 29, 1938 at Pomona, California and adopted five weeks later. We moved to Hermosa Beach when I was four. Fishing began with my Mom and Dad in Mammoth Creek and I became an expert by age six. At age seven I was fishing by myself on Manhattan Beach Pier with a five-foot steel baitcast rod and reel. I put a tin can on the front axle of my bike to hold the rod butt and gripped the shaft on the handlebar. Walleyed perch were my specialty and a sort of Lucky Joe setup with four-hook leader and a shiny sinker was dropped near the pilings. The area where I fished is now sanded in and waves break beyond the end of the pier.

Next, I began going on the fishing barges BONNIE K., RETRIEVER, MANANA, and BUCCANEER. The fare to fish on the barges was $2.50 at that time. A customer could go from one barge to another free and I spent all day doing just that. I would also go to Redondo and ride the shoreboat AVENGER for 50 cents, just for the boat ride. My Dad began taking my friends and me on the half-day boats at Redondo: GW, MAIDEN LINDA LEE and CITY OF REDONDO. Trips were also made from Newport and San Clemente with L.A.

County lifeguard Dick Evans, who liked fishing as much as I did. We went from Port Orange on ALALUNGA, MISSAWIT, MAY B., and SEABISCUIT and caught lots of bass, barracuda and albacore. Free passes for fishing from Pierpoint Landing were won from the popular "Fishing Flashes" television show.

When I was 12 years old I got a job mowing grass at the home of Bruce Barnes in Manhattan Beach. One day he asked me if I liked to fish. My answer was "Yes!" I knew he was skipper of the sport boat ISLAND QUEEN. He had just gotten a new job as captain of the STAR ANGLER at Joe Martin's 22nd Street Landing in San Pedro. It was the four a.m. all-day boat fishing local or Catalina, wherever it was best. Every morning during the summer Bruce would pick me up at the corner by my house at three A.M. I guess I was what they call a "pinhead" these days. I was a cleanup boy and during the next two years I learned how to fish, chum, gaff, clean fish, steer the boat, pull and drop the anchor, clean the galley stove top for free food, paint the bilges and take abuse from obnoxious passengers.

Bruce was a good teacher and he gave me a new fiberglass rod called a "Spin-cutta." He got free rods as samples. Riding home with a friend who was old enough to drive, I had the pole sticking out a window. It clipped a tree and snapped in two. Heartbroken, I told

Bruce about the accident and he said I could have another one, but I would have to earn it. I think I worked 1,000 hours for those poles. I still have that rod to this day, 53 years later. I can cast a jig 50 yards and when I take it on a party boat everyone looks at me like I am a geek. If I offer to let them try it out, they run away.

This photo of my 22 1/2 pound white seabass appeared in the Redondo Daily Breeze *on July 12, 1951. Fish was caught on sportboat LINDA LEE. I was 12 years old.*

I learned to row a boat by paddling around a trout lake all day.

Right: I fished on the GW at Redondo.

I went fishing on the CITY OF REDONDO and hooked this 25-pound halibut with 10-pound test line and a spinning rod I made myself.

Bait catchers at Long Beach:COUR D'ALENE, SUNBEAM II, NEREID, JACKIE BOY, URANUS, GARY.

Bait Catcher

When I was 15 I had a chance to work on the bait boat DONNA K that was owned by Joe Martin. I took the job as it paid big money, $10 a night, which was about 60 cents an hour. I got paid every Monday in $1 bills and always had a big roll of money (dollar bills). I learned a lot and liked it better than the party boats. The captain was Herb Muller, who at that time had white hair. I thought he was very old, but he is alive today in his late 80s, I know now some people get gray hair early in life. His son has the REDONDO SPECIAL at Redondo Sportfishing.

Herb's brothers-in-law were a couple of house carpenters, the Becking boys, who built the CATHIE J. in Manhattan Beach. The boat was used as a bait transport to sell to private and charter boats. I sometimes worked on her and on weekends the Becking brothers liked to take the boat and play captains. They didn't know much and, even though the CATHIE J. carried many automobile tires as side fenders, were fearful of other boats crashing into her. The bait tanks were mostly below deck level and when loaded the boat had only about two feet of freeboard at the stern. On the aft side of the stern tank was a four-foot sign "BAIT." The Beckings wanted us deckhands to hold off boats coming alongside with our feet. It is a good way to lose a leg and I wouldn't do it. They didn't like that.

One of our regular customers had a surplus Navy LCPL spoonbill landing craft for a charter boat. The bow on a spoonbill has no stem from the deck and curves under to the waterline. One night he was approaching the CATHIE J. to pick up bait and I could see the skipper was in trouble. He yelled, "No reverse!" He was heading straight for the stern and the Beckings hollered, "Hold her off!" I ran up behind the cabin and the spoonbill came up over the stern and broke the bait sign. There was about eight feet from the stern to the bait tank and the charter boat sat there like a seine skiff on a tuna boat. He finally got the shift in reverse and, after many tries, backed her off the CATHIE J. If I had tried to hold her off as the Beckings wanted me to do, I would have been crushed flat. When they saw me flee forward, they started running toward the stern to push off, but they were too late. I hoped they realized how lucky they were.

In the 1950s and '60s numerous sportfishing landings were based in the Los Angeles Harbor area from Cabrillo Beach in San Pedro, to Wilmington and Long Beach. Private boats were also numerous. All these boats needed live bait and the larger landings owned their own bait catchers or had contract bait boats. Some of the San Pedro bait boats I remember are: DONNA K, CATHIE J, O&K, SUNSHINE II, STANDARD, PEER, FIGHTING BOB, and SEA HAWK. In Long Beach: GARY, JACKIE BOY, URANUS, NEREID, SUNBEAM, and CITY OF LONG BEACH. Live bait sold for a standard $2 a scoop, 50 cents to commercial fishermen, and there were a lot of special deals in between. About ten bait catcher boats were working in the harbor. Those boats that weren't under contract sold bait to the public and competition was intense.

97

CATHIE J. had many fenders on her sides.

LCPL like this ran over the stern of the CATHIE J.

Not all of them got along with each other and as I look back it is amazing no one got killed. The cotton bait net webbing was fragile and there were cases of nets being ruined with acid. Light skiffs were sunk. A boat would go alongside a skiff and pour water in with the deck hose, or let the overflow water from the bait tank run in until the skiff had a low freeboard, and then sneak away in the dark. The first large wake that came along would sink the skiff and it happened to the DONNA K. skiffs a couple of times.

We had a problem with a certain boat and took care of it with an old ice cream freezer salvaged from a grocery store. We filled it with concrete, fixed 4x4s to protrude from the top, wrapped them with barbed wire, and dumped it under one of his light skiffs. That night we were hovering nearby to see the result. A market boat called the intended victim and asked permission to make a set on the skiff as it had a lot of fish under it. He got the go ahead and we knew it would be a disaster, but could not say a word. The market boat hung up solid and did considerable damage to his net. We felt really bad.

A good friend at the time was a bosn's mate in the Coast Guard and operator of a 41-foot harbor patrol boat. One night he came alongside and tied up for a visit. One of our crew asked if he could take the patrol boat for a little spin. My friend gave the okay and away he went, heading straight for a light skiff belonging to the boat for whom we had built the freezer snag. He circled the enemy skiff at 20 knots, throwing a big wake in hopes of sending it to the bottom. Our man came back and tied up, a big smile on his face. As he was on his joy ride around this skiff, I saw drifting in the dark the owner of the skiff, observing the whole scene. My friend could be in deep doodoo for allowing a civilian to use the patrol boat, especially for mischief. He took off and never came near us again. The light skiff didn't sink and, as the Coastie did not get in trouble, the infraction was apparently never reported. The caper opened some eyes on our side for sure.

Billy Rice had a bait receiver moored between the San Pedro lighthouse and Cabrillo Beach and also sold bait directly from his boat. Paul Froude on the O&K caught bait for Norm's Landing in San Pedro and would sometimes anchor between the receiver and the main channel and attempt to intercept Billy's customers. One morning, after being asked not to do it, Rice came

The bait boat DONNA K.

Mike, at left, steering the DONNA K.

alongside the O&K to invite Paul aboard the SUNSHINE II for a drink. Froude liked a good drink and jumped aboard the SUNSHINE. Billy pulled away and had one of his husky crew beat the hell out of Paul and put him back aboard his boat. O&K never again anchored in front of the receiver.

These incidents are just a few of those that occurred. It was just business, you know. A few of the players involved are still around. Actually, those were the good times for the bait boats. Not one of that live bait fleet is afloat today and I doubt that there is that much competition now. Only the currently working boat crews know.

Each boat had its loyal customers. Capt. Billy Rice on the SUNSHINE II had many very faithful customers. For those that sold bait from their boats a good place to anchor was by the red dolphin at the entrance to Cerritos Channel, near the federal prison. The first bait boat to arrive got the first position, the second boat got the second, and so on. Many times the CATHIE J. had the Number One spot and we would blink the spotlight to attract the private boats coming from the marinas in Wilmington. No matter where Billy was in the line of bait boats, nothing could entice his customers away from the SUNSHINE II. Their loyalty was amazing. They would call on the AM radio asking where he was. He would reply that he was waiting just for them with bait in his tank, and sign off, "SUNSHINE II, WB 3439, Out." He always had a bottle of Canadian Club whiskey if the customers needed a drink and many of them enjoyed it.

Billy's bait scoops had very limber wooden handles

Preparing to start the generator on a light skiff.

that would bend noticeably, giving the appearance of a large, heavy load of bait. Our scoops averaged 12-14 pounds of bait, Billy's were more like 10 pounds. He would occasionally take a couple meshes out of the scoop, making it more shallow. We would sometimes offer bait at half price, two for one, but no luck with his customers. He was a hell of a salesman. In the 1930s he was one of the most famous and well-advertised sportfishing skippers and the popularity he acquired evidently carried over to his postwar bait business.

The late Tony West worked for Billy and one afternoon when they were starting up their light skiffs Rice was drunk and ran the SUNSHINE into the breakwater, causing her to sink. Tony got tangled in the rigging and almost didn't make it to the rescue skiff. The boat was raised, repaired and soon back in business.

Three brothers: Popeye, Jimmy, and Ronnie Bunn worked several years for Billy Rice. He offered a full share or so much a night as pay. Some men opted for the share, but if they quit or were let go before the season ended, they got nothing. The season was from Memorial Day to Labor Day. On the DONNA K. we were paid every Monday with a share-out sheet listing the check from Joe Martin for his party boat bait and big stacks of one dollar bills from the cash sales. I never felt I was getting shortchanged.

Most of the bait boats had a row of car tires hanging on the sides to absorb the hits they received almost daily from boats coming alongside. Captain Billy Rice had his famous old SUNSHINE II hung with two rows of white-painted tires in addition to a 6"x12" guard rail along the sides and around the stern. I once saw the RADAR, a 30-foot Monterey boat, ram his side at a 90 degree angle running about three knots.

A DONNA K light skiff in tow.

SUNSHINE II was a popular sportboat in the 1930s.

SUNSHINE II as a postwar bait catcher.

The RADAR hit and began sinking immediately. There was no damage to Billy's heavy guard rail. Another believer in stout guard rails was Bill Odette at Newport Beach. His BILLY BOY had massive rails especially to protect the sides. The boat is still catching bait for Virge's Landing in Morro Bay. Art Mello's MONA LIZA, built in the 1950s, was the first steel-hulled bait catcher I remember. Compared to wooden boats, steel boats are fairly safe. MONA LIZA is still catching live bait at Marina Del Rey.

Nearly all the bait-catching boats used light skiffs at night to attract anchovies and sardines. The skiffs were kept clear of the ship channels and anchored inside the breakwater in areas where the bottom was free of snags. Each boat had its favorite spots and it was not a good idea to poach on them. Some spots were very small and had a clean bottom the size of one net, maybe 175 feet around. At that time no GPS plotters or radars were available to fishboats. AM radios and flashing Fathometers were the only electronic aids. In daylight all the skiffs were anchored at their chosen spots using landmarks, lining up buildings, bridges, and other stationary features. Lights on channel buoys or shore were used at night.

I learned all these marks and when as I worked my way up on the DONNA K. and ended up being the guy who went out in the afternoon and started up the generators on the seven light skiffs that were anchored around San Pedro-Long Beach Harbor. I learned the snags on the bottom, which we had to avoid. We had a list each evening of where to move skiffs according to where bait fish were found. I would get the lights going

O&K competed with the SUNSHINE II for bait sales.

and be back at the dock about a half hour before dark. I often ate dinner at Tony's Cafe at Beacon Streets in San Pedro. Beacon Street was a lively place and I enjoyed roaming around there even if I was too young to take advantage of the possibilities is offered.

The whole crew of four or five men would arrive about 10 P.M. and we would get underway and cruise to the nearest light skiff and check it with the fathometer. If it looked good I would be dropped off in the skiff with a set of long oars. The anchor would be slowly pulled

My first boat, the FAMIGLIA G., later SANTA ANNA.

and I held the skiff steady with the oars while the DONNA K. circled it, paying out the net. As the wings were pulled, I would keep the skiff centered in the net until it was almost up and then row over the corks and tie the corkline to the skiff to keep it high so the bait would not escape. If we had more bait than needed to fill the tanks on the DONNA K. two long poles would be hooked to the bow and stern of the skiff to hold it away from the big boat and form a large bag that gave the bait more swimming room. As we waited on the anchor, the sportboats would come alongside and pick up their bait. Sometimes we could bait six to ten boats in a couple of sets, at other times it required seven or eight sets to get the job done.

From July to September, after baiting up the sports, we would go to Fish Harbor in the early morning and sell salted anchovies in five gallon cans to the albacore jig boats from Washington and Oregon. They came in season to fish the Mexican waters and some took as

Scooping mackerel at night.

many as 20 or 30 cans. They always came back with a better catch than the boats that did not chum their jigs with the salt bait. We also sold live bait to the smaller bait boats.

My First Boats and Barracuda Trolling

I saved my money, but also passed up some good jobs fishing for albacore. When I finished high school in 1956 I bought the 30-foot Monterey boat the FAMIGLIA G. from Manuel Robello, a retired tuna fisherman from San Diego, who had her to fish out his senior years. I paid $2,000 with a lot of trolling gear and setlines included, and changed the name to SANTA ANNA.

Beginning in the Spring, I trolled for barracuda until September, from Oceanside to Malibu. Bone jigs on three weighted lines were the lures. Another favorite was a lure designed by Jim Putters, a famous old-time fisherman at Redondo. The "Putters Jig" was aluminum, poured at the Alcast Foundry and patterned after a bone jig. We had to provide our own wobble rings and single hooks. We usually painted them white, with maybe a touch of red or blue. The barracuda soon chewed the paint off, so frequent repainting was required.

As a deckhand on the sport boats I saw how the barracuda trollers often circled too closely around them and knew how that worked. I knew also that the captains would shoot at any sea lions that turned up. In those days some of the passengers carried pistols and would do the same. (I think some preferred seal shooting more than the fishing). The bullets would ricochet across the water and at times I could hear them whizzing by. Not a good thing.

I was also aware that most party boats had someone to throw a line-cutter at the jig boats. This was a 3/4" pipe, 8 or 10 inches long with two pieces of 1/8" flat bar welded to the end like a rocket tail. They were razor sharp. I could cast one a long way and tried hard to cut those bad jig boat lines. I got a few, I am sorry to say, but was only doing what I was told. Anyway, I knew enough to stay out of range when I was fishing around the party boat fleet. It is possible to catch a lot of barracuda without the benefit of sportboat chumlines and I learned to do it. I would call my friends to come when I found the fish and they reciprocated and called me into their hot spots.

In the winters I worked on other boats fishing for mackerel, squid, white seabass and rock cod. I also crewed on albacore bait boats in the summer, fishing from Mexico to Eureka. In the latter part of the summer we spent a lot of time working off the coast from Monterey to Morro Bay.

101

The JOE was somewhat unstable.

One of the fishing methods I learned at an early age was scooping mackerel. It was with Bud Austin on his Kettenburg WINIFRED II. We ranged from Malibu to Newport and Catalina, fishing mostly at night, and delivered to the Coast cannery in Wilmington. Many types and sizes of boats were scooping, some being junk.

In 1958 I bought JOE, my second boat for $1,500, only because I needed a boat and couldn't find anything better at the time. JOE was a 30-foot double-ender, similar to a Monterey, but with a round bottom that didn't ride anything like a Monterey. I jigged barracuda all summer and as fall came around the mackerel boats began making good catches. Having almost rolled over a couple of times with a ton of barries in the hold, I knew the JOE was unstable and needed careful handling. I lined the hold with plywood and made it watertight to carry mackerel with seawater and ice, This would also allow unloading at the cannery with the big pumps they had instead of shoveling by hand.

Mackerel were bringing $50 a ton and the cannery was furnishing free chum in 55-gallon drums. I got two drums, which was plenty for me. JOE held 2 ¾ tons of mackerel in the hold, but I was afraid to put more on deck as the boat would go down fast.

I began fishing along the coast and one day I got a tip that purse seiners had found a lot of fish at Santa Barbara Island. It was 49 miles from San Pedro, a long run for me, but as few other scoop boats knew about it chances of loading up were good. It was twice as far as I had ever gone in the JOE, but the weather was good and I was almost fearless, so off I went.

I got to the island after dark and began looking around. A couple of seiners and one scoop boat were already there. I made a chum line away from that boat and the mackerel came up heavy. I anchored and chummed a little and saw there was no current, but there was a lot of fish coming in from all directions.

That is not good for scooping, but I quickly filled the boat and was on my way home. It was the most fish I had ever put in the JOE and thanks to a calm sea, I made it back to San Pedro with the bow up in the air and the stern under water. In a sloppy sea it would have been a different story.

I wondered how much the other scoop boat had caught, as it was larger and had a crew of three. They came in as I was leaving the cannery and it was the MARILENE F. with George and Benny Fukuzaki. They had scooped 15 tons of mackerel that night, which was to me unheard of, but they were highliners in any fishery they tried. I figured I was lucky with my 2 ¾ tons and had better not go out there again in case my luck ran out. As it was, the NW wind came up and the fish disappeared.

Next I got word of fish near Santa Monica and when I arrived there were 15 boats already there and fishing as the sun went down. I anchored and nearby and began chumming, but an hour after dark a NE wind began to blow. That is an offshore direction in that area and it blew hard. Some boats took off for Pedro and I followed. It became too rough to go to Rocky Point so I tried for the Redondo breakwater. That course was no good as the wind was on the beam. Heading for Rocky Point, the further I went the rougher it got. As the sea was on my stern, twice the JOE spun completely around and was heading back the way I had come. The 1,000 pounds of weight on deck in the 55-gallon chum barrels made the boat top-heavy and it scared the heck out of me, but I made it to San Pedro.

The next day I talked to some of the old veteran Santa Monica Bay fishermen and found they had made good catches by remaining at anchor. The offshore wind does not build any big sea in close. "How come you

Load of scooped mackerel. Note chum barrels on stern.

102

MAYFLOWER was once used by Gilbert Van Camp as his private yacht.

didn't stay right where you were?" they asked. I didn't know then, but I sure do now. A person can learn something new every day that he fishes.

I sold the JOE after that night. One fisherman wanted to buy it on easy credit and pay as you go. He got really irate when I said no. The cannery ceased buying mackerel the next week and I would never have gotten paid. The principal of Washington High School in Los Angeles bought the boat for sportfishing. I told him when he was cruising around the air would be fresher if he would keep the front window in the pilot house open and sit by it. I didn't mention that he might get gassed by the engine fumes. He ran the boat into a big bunker barge in Cerritos Channel and barely made it to a nearby marina dock where he could tie up and not sink. He got it to John's Boat Shop and it wound up in different storage yards around Wilmington. About 10 years later someone nailed plywood all over the hull and I thought maybe JOE would see the ocean again, but it never did. My next boat, in 1959, was ROSE MARIE, a 32-foot Monterey with a Caterpillar engine and a good refrigeration system. With her I did some swordfishing and other ventures.

Tuna Clipper Days

My next job was working for Gilbert Van Camp on the MAYFLOWER, a 135-foot tuna bait boat owned by the Van Camp cannery. She was powered by a 1,000 hp Union diesel and auxiliary engines and could carry 350 tons of tuna. Gilbert used it as his private yacht and to take prospective customers on fishing trips.

Gilbert Van Camp in 1960.

103

My job was to help in the engine room, clean the boat, and work in the galley. More importantly, I was in charge of all the fishing gear. I made up the commercial gear such as the "squids" and live bait rigs and secured them to the bamboo poles. I also maintained the sport tackle that we used.

We would buy 1,000 scoops of live bait from Bill Dugan on the CITY OF LONG BEACH that fished for Pierpoint Landing, of which Gilbert was part owner. We would cruise down to Mexico and fish for yellowtail, black skipjack, yellowfin tuna, albacore and skipjack that we delivered to the cannery after each trip.

Gilbert loved to fish and was good at it, but was really hyper. He would get very upset if we weren't catching fish. Captain Art Sousa would tell him to go to his cabin and not come out until we stopped on fish. Gilbert got the corner rack and special chumming so he would catch the most fish. Every time he caught one the crew yelled, "Aattaboy Gilbert!" I had to fish the side away from the guests and never got an "Attaboy."

Gilbert insisted the guests fish all day and for many it was the first time and they got wet and tired and did not enjoy it. No one was permitted to sit out a stop and I think a lot of the guests went home pissed off and never bought any tuna.

Gilbert also loved to play jokes. I once caught a very large mahi-mahi (dorado) on sport tackle. When I held it up it was as long as I was tall: 6'3". Photos were taken for the "Fishing Flashes" TV show and the fish was barbecued for dinner. Everyone was at the table with fish on their plates when Gilbert opened a can of Van Camp sardines in mustard sauce. He stirred them up and poured them on top of his dolphin fish, chewed a mouthful and then drooled it slowly out of his mouth and onto his plate. A few of the guests got up and ran outside to lose their dinners over the side. Gilbert just laughed and laughed. He was quite a guy.

Ulitmate Boats

I sold my Monterey to Vince Quincey in San Diego and in 1964 bought a 36-foot boat put together by the famous Ditmar-Donaldson yard in Costa Mesa. Named PIEFACE, she was built for a schoolteacher for summer albacore fishing. The teacher fished her for 10 years before I got her, but I didn't realize she was almost new when I bought her. I still have her 43 years later and she is still not really old, as wooden fishing boats go. Many are over 60 and my third Monterey is 80 years old. Remember, you can fix a boat if you spend the money. Unlike boats, sick people, even millionaires, cannot always be saved.

The little PIEFACE is a good boat. The first owner

Jig boat layout.

liked Kettenburg boats, which with the right owners were real money-makers in the '40s-'60s. Kettenburg built 80 38-ft boats and four 32-ft. boats. PIEFACE is 35 feet long, but carries the same amount of fuel as the 38-footers, which hold 10-12 tons of albacore. Including two deck tanks of 105 gallons each, PIEFACE holds 670 gallons of fuel. That's a lot for a 35-foot boat. It is built stronger than Kettennburg boats with heavier ribs, deck beams, etc. I can fish for all types of fish and have gear for all of them: albacore, bonito, salmon, rock cod, barracuda, white seabass gillnets, trawl halibut, sea cucumbers and lampara net.

For trolling I have my third Monterey, THERESA ANN, purchased in 1995. I use her for salmon, bonito,

My second Monterey on the slipways.

PIEFACE today.

THERESA ANNE rigged for salmon trolling.

barracuda, etc. I sometimes alternate from one boat to the other. I think being able to fish for whatever is available and profitable is a must, which also means you need to have the permits.

Without the limited entry permits a person is short-changed and can only watch as other fishermen make money. Back in the '30's to the '50s, one just bought a boat registration and commercial license and went fishing. Nowadays it is a totally different story. Some boats did not fish for a certain fish for a few years. When lim-

ited entry was introduced a permit was granted only to those who had landed X amount of that species during those years. If one missed the qualifying years, he was out of luck, even if he had 30 years in the fishery. Somehow that is not right, but that is the way it is.

During my lifetime of fishing I have had some a great catches and being one who is always looking for a better way to fish, or a way to start a new fishery, I have had some very poor catches, but if you don't try then how do you know?

The versatile PIEFACE.

Boating a harpooned swordfish.

ROSE MARIE cruising for swordfish.

Chapter 8
SPEARING SWORDFISH

One of the fisheries I most enjoyed was for broadbill swordfish. I started out with my friend Freddy Young on his Murray-hulled boat BREEZY. We built two big boxes on deck to hold iced fish. Freddy had fished a few months on another boat and learned a little about swordfishing. I knew nothing. We spent the summer around Catalina and Santa Barbara Island and caught 35 fish.

On one of our first trips we anchored at Long Point, Catalina Island. A guy named Arnold Silva came by in his fantail boat ARNETTA. He wanted to know who we were and if we knew anything about swordfish. We admitted being new at it and he proceeded to clue us in on the proper way to fish. "Look for chopped up kelp. The swordfish chop it up trying to eat the small fish hiding in it. Look for fins sticking out of the water. Don't go near any boats that are looking for fish. Don't pull a fish until it is dead." And a few more good tips I can't remember.

Out we went and found chopped kelp and caught a fish. All a sudden there was Arnold cruising around real close to us. It seemed as if we were doing OK, but that the ARNETTA was always trying to get our fish. We learned later that is something that is just not done.

A few years later on my own boat I learned how to make a very good dummy out of swordfish fins and I slipped one out for Arnold, who was trying to get a fish we had run, but not harpooned. We faked it and ran a nothing fish, stopping to look for it just before slipping out the dummy. Here comes Arnold as we were stopped waiting for the fish to come up. One of the unwritten rules at that time was if you stop and don't move much, the fish is yours and other boats are supposed to give you first chance at the fish when it reappears. Arnold spots the dummy, speeds up and runs out on the plank to spear the fish. I turned and speeded up just to make him nervous. He ran wide-open and almost threw at the dummy. Back on the bridge he said over the radio, "That sure was a good-looking dummy." After that he didn't mess with us anymore.

A large fleet of boats chased swordfish every year. Some were part-timers, but many worked year-around and fished swordfish along with other fisheries. They sailed from all the harbors from Santa Barbara to San Diego. Starting from San Pedro, I was in the middle and fished mostly from outside that port to the Santa Barbara Islands, Catalina and San Clemente.

One thing I noticed when the Santa Barbara boats came to Catalina was that they carried 50-75 pound anchors and lots of chain. The San Pedro and Newport boats had 30-pound anchors and mostly rope. They never anchored at Catalina, just tied up to moorings scattered

Arnold Silva's ARNETTA.

around the island. I had never been to the northern Channel Islands except when passing by on an albacore boat, but when I moved to Santa Barbara I found out why the boats had heavy anchor gear. Winds of 30-50 mph are not uncommon around the Channel Islands. It was amusing to see the inexperienced yachtsmen trying to cope with a stiff blow; their dinghies would capsize, canvas bridge canopies would rip apart and anchors would drag. One experience with a high wind and some of the yachts never again visited the islands

Every port believed it had the most swordfish highliners. Newport had several successful boats: ALERT, BUDDY, REFUGE, NEPTUNE, CRYSTAL SEA, LOUISE, JAMA-JAN, and JEAN LOUISE to name a few. New boats came and went over the years and even yachts began to fit planks for harpooning. Elmer Herr's DORSAL was one of the first, Elmer got bored with catching marlin and began spearing swordfish for fun. His skipper was old-timer sport captain Sammy Cordeiro. They got a lot of fish and would race commercial boats to

fish, which we did not think was fair. Yachts using planks led to the use of airplanes for spotting fish.

Elmer had sonar and could track fish maybe five to fifteen feet underwater, within harpoon range. He took a couple of fish that we found that went down when we ran them. We would drift and wait for them to come up finning again. The Dorsal approached and slowly circled us and then Sammy would be on the plank and throw the harpoon. It would go deep and we could see it hit the fish. A sonar was on my wish list also, but they had a high price and my boat lacked room in the bow for the necessary transducer sea chest. I now have one with two small transducers, one on each side of the keel. It has a 2,400-foot range, but 600 feet is plenty for swordfish.

Bob Hitt and his wife Mary built the fiberglass CRYSTAL SEA from a plaster of Paris mold. Bob was a skilled craftsman and worked for Dittmar in the winters. He had many stories, some pretty farfetched. He once told me that there were two kinds of swordfish: razorbacks and humpbacks. The first are long and skinny with narrow backs, thin bacon and large stomach cavities. Humpbacks average larger with thick bacon, small stomach cavities, and are wide and flat with a sort of groove in the middle. I began watching for these features and found that Bob was right. The large fish that dress out at 450-500 pounds are mostly humpbacks.

When there are good numbers of fish of 200-250 pounds cleaned in an area they are humpbacks, so I believe they travel in schools more than razorbacks. From what I have seen, there seems to be two types of swordfish, but when I mention it to people I get funny looks.

Bobby once said he was watching a sailboat with his binoculars and saw the reflection of a finning swordfish in the sail. He ran toward the sailboat and stuck the fish. He also claimed that instead of backing

Babe Castagnola ready to harpoon a swordie.

Bob Hitt's CRYSTAL SEA.

Finning swordfish.

into the wind while pulling the fish by hand, he would tie it off to the boat and run ahead until the fish came floating to the surface where he could back up to it pulling slack line. Next day we passed him outside the harbor hauling a fish straight up from the bottom. It was risky, putting a lot of strain on the fish unless he knew the for certain that it was "button holed." That is when the dart goes all the way through and comes out the other side.

He once found an underwater fish on the Mackerel Bank inside San Clemente and got over it, but it as too deep to harpoon. The fish was swimming toward the bank on the east end of Catalina so he told Mary to follow. It took a couple of hours, but when the fish came to the shallower water of the bank, perhaps from 300 to

Beadle and John Peterson boating a swordfish.

100 fathoms, it surfaced within range and he stuck it. All I can say is if Bob and Mary were out there today they would catch more than their share of fish.

Author's Note: Mike's swordfishing memoir regarding Bob Hitt: Ed Ries knew him shortly after the end of World War II when he was transferred to the submarine tender USS BUSHNELL (AS 15). Ed was leading petty officer in charge of the First Division of the deck force, and Hitt was one of 63 seamen assigned to the division. The ship was underway on a cruise to Guam when the two men discovered they had a common link to the fishing community in Newport Beach. Many hours were passed "shooting the breeze" about the fishing they both knew. Contact was lost when Hitt was sent home for discharge and Ed stayed on as a Navy regular. Mike's story furnishes an account of Hitt's later occupation as a successful commercial fisherman.

Shortly after the movie *Jaws* was released we were off the Fishhook at San Clemente Island and harpooned a fish that had a stainless steel shaft in its back, near the tail. About a foot was showing and it turned out be from a harpoon gun, same as the type used in the movie, except instead of being attached to a rope, the remains of a small nylon cord, 96-thread or less, were tied to the collar. The line had chafed off so they lost the fish, which never knew it was stuck and just kept swimming around. It weighed 385 pounds, cleaned. I still have that shaft on the PIEFACE and it is one of the extras that will go with the boat when I sell it. It is too bad there isn't a swordfish museum where I eould auction it off.

Swordfishing takes a good team of two people and one of the best was Dave and Herb Gale on the GORDITO. Art Killion and Junior Nilson on the MONTALVO were another duo and I could name many more. I think Santa Barbara had some of the best swordfish boats on the coast. They outfished anyone who came to the Channel Islands and did well anywhere they went. Some of the old-time boats I remember were C.H., EL SOLE, SAL C., SVANA, EAGLE B, REMORA, MARY K, TWO SONS, OGENIO, SANTA LUCIA, VINCENT K., SAVOIA and more.

One day in the early '70s we came out of Cat Harbor on Catalina Island and I headed up toward the West End. My plan was to go up one to one and a half miles off the island and then run out a few more miles to a high spot. The other boats in the harbor had gone in different directions so we were alone. Just before we got to the West End we spotted a swordfish and "put him in the water" (harpooned it). We searched around the area and harpooned three more fish. This was at the time when everyone had or wanted to have an airplane spotting fish for him. Anyone

Art Killion cleaning a swordfish

that had a flying friend had him searching for fish. There were some really poor fliers over the ocean.

I heard an engine and looked up and here came this young hot dog pilot in a Catabria with green stripes on the wings. I had seen him before and he was bad news for any other planes around him. He spotted our flags and circled our area. We caught four more fish and as we were making an approach he would dive bomb us, passing very close trying to make us screw up and miss the fish.

Seven cleaned swordfish.

He was known to use a lot of drugs and I feared he would kill himself and us also with his reckless flying.

I knew he had called his boat to come and about 45 minutes later it came over the horizon steaming at full speed towards us. We now had eight fish in the water and the other swordfish had gone down for the day so they did not catch any as they went through our gear. The plane dived on us a few more times, coming dangerously close to our crow's nest. The next week he crashed and was killed. As I watched guys like him I knew it was only a matter of time.

Hitt's first boat

Harpooning was a good fishery that began around May first every year and sometimes lasted until Thanksgiving. It depended on water temperature and weather. Rain and southeast winds usually came in November and shut it off. One year we fished between Newport 14-Mile Bank and Dana Point from the last of October until 12 days before Thanksgiving and took 78 fish. A strong southeast wind came up on Thanksgiving Day and the fish disappeared. An old-timer once told me that fish don't move, the water moves. Fish always stay in water where they are happy, and I feel after all these years of fishing, it was a very true statement.

The best year I had we caught 286 swordfish, maybe 10 of those with aid of an airplane. We got 125 fish one year while most boats stayed tied up because of the mercury scare. Each fish was supposed to be tested after it was landed. I would send in 25-30 pieces of fish to be tested, go out and start getting fish. We found that bonito shark worked very well for the tests. In the middle of the trip I would check in to see how many passed. Usually it was about three-quarters, so we would get that amount plus some more. We would put a test paper with

SANTA LUCIA

Swordfish buoys attached to dart lines.

each fish and the market would sell them.

The price was good with a test, the rest the market bought at a lower price. The whole thing was a sham. We would go to Santa Cruz and start looking and get seven or eight fish a day, no problem. It was the same at all the islands. After we got our "quota" we would head for San Pedro and pass finning fish all afternoon until dark. It would have been the biggest year in history if all the boats could have fished.

I was thinking the other day about how many fish we caught with the little PIEFACE in a few short years. It was around 1,000. We caught enough swordfish in a special spot at Santa Cruz Island that it became known as "McCorkle's Garden." I am not sure why, but Dario Castagnola was the first to call it that. No one else could beat our catches at that spot. Now you go out and spear a fish and there are two to four airplanes over you in a few minutes and a big yacht under them.

When I was harpooning on my Monterey ROSE MARIE some fishermen would leave their fish on deck overnight, covered with burlap, to let them cool off and save ice. Old-timer Babe Castagnola told me, "Don't leave fish uncovered during a full moon because they will get soft." I believed him, but I had refrigeration and put them straight in the hold after cleaning them.

PIEFACE has an extra-long "plank."

Bob Hitt pulling a swordfish.

BREEZY

ESQUIRE and JAMA JAN.

ROSE MARIE was a nice Monterey boat a and a good troller for albacore.

PIEFACE rigged for albacore with trolling poles and bait tank.

Chapter 9
ALBACORE

If modern sport-recreational anglers had to fish the way old-time commercial albacore fishermen did most would be lost and out of luck. Until the 1960s small boats navigated with only a simple box compass and a timepiece. As boats were running all day, usually on many different courses, and then drifting at night at the whim of winds and currents often moving in opposite directions, location was by guesswork. After WWII, most boats could add AM radios with two channels, 2638 and 2738, that greatly improved safety and ability to exchange up-to-date fishing information. Albacore boats worked in a fleet that covered a large area that was moving constantly to stay with migrating longfins. Depending on the speed of the albacore travels, in a week the fleet could move 50-100 miles. Many fishermen just followed the fleet without paying much attention to where they were and when it was time to head for port would ask for directions from other boats or by listening on their radios.

Another very useful tool was the radio direction finder, or "DF" as it was called. It enabled a skipper to take bearings on shore beacons such as Point Loma and San Pedro lights. Two or more bearings could provide a fix on his location that could be marked on a navigation chart.

If the signal was broadcast long enough, bearings could also be taken of transmissions from other boats that were catching fish. For fishermen, this was the most useful feature of the DF, but it took a little time to swing the loop and if the message was short the direction was often missed. Eventually, automatic direction finders that pointed instantly at any signal, were available. I had a Raytheon that would get a boat in San Francisco when I was at the dock in San Pedro.

Because of varying AM signal strengths, it was difficult to tell how far away the sender was. Sometimes, hearing of a good bite, boats would get a bearing and take off running for what they supposed would be one or two hours away when in fact it was six hours and nightfall was in two hours. The invention of the "S" meter for the DFs helped with the problem by showing the distance to a signal source.

Chasing "radio fish" could be tricky as the reports were not always true. A few gullible captains ran after them and got the banana. Some boats that held 10 tons at times reported that many fish in one stop. Or, "Had

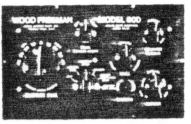
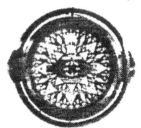
1983 ad for an a late model of autopilot.

a good stop for two tons." Same the next day, and on succeeding days until their reported catch would add up to 15-20 tons and then they would unload only six tons at the cannery.

Another labor-saving device that made life easier for commercial fishermen was the automatic pilot, or autopilot. Fishing by himself in a trolling boat, Wood Freeman found it difficult to pull fish and steer the boat at the same time. In 1935 he worked to build a mechanism that could accurately steer the boat on a preset course while he caught fish. So successful was he that within a few years his invention became standard in well-equipped boats.

A bunch of Northwest salmon trollers would come south for albacore and their Norwegian owners kept together. Using their autopilots they would tack up and down the swell on straight courses, a different procedure from California boats that usually circled when fish were biting. I would hear them on the AM radio, "Ya, you betcha Ole, I'm heading south-southwest and have her on de Iron Mike."

I didn't have a clue. Was this some kind of code? Fishermen had codes and I still have a tuna clipper code sheet. Then I would hear, "She's on the Mike." It had to be a code. I could hear the boat engine noise in the background and a mysterious grinding noise, which I later learned was the pilot motor "hunting." I also learned that Mike and Iron Mike referred to the Wood Freeman autopilot.

I remember when I first went albacore fishing the captain would show me how to change course with the autopilot when I had the wheel watch. I was shown how to take it out of gear, change course and put it back in gear. The Wood Freeman autopilot was the "hunting" type that went back and forth to keep the boat on its preset course. Because it was very important the compass stayed dry, it was often covered and even had a light shining on it for warmth. As the machines were covered, I didn't know what they really looked like or how they worked.

I now have two Wood Freeman autopilots, one on each of my boats. They are old, but I can buy or rebuild the motors, which are rumored to be old-time Dodge starter motors. The clutch is heavy cast bronze that will last 100 years and the compass is mounted on an unbreakable bronze yoke. They came with a troubleshooting book and are easy to repair, although they do have a few quirks. Over the years I have learned how to keep them going and I have no desire to switch to a newer, hi-tech model. If it needed repairing, for $100 a technician would tell me it needed a new main board, or a new motor or, "Just buy a new one as they don't make parts for this model anymore". For my Model 12 Wood Freeman pilots I have spare brushes for the motors and I clean the points in the "brain box" once in a while.

Without the autopilots, life would be a lot harder and I am glad Wood Freeman had the skill to invent something that has benefited thousands of fishermen. Old timers like me, who are satisfied with proven technology will keep using the dependable "Iron Mike" for years to come. When I was on the HAPPY III fishing

HAPPY III.

near Guadalupe, I was always curious about the identity of other boats we saw. Ole would tell me and I would log it in my brain. I soon became good at remembering who was who and if they were on the fishing grounds, something I believe is a very important part of catching fish. For example: if you hear someone made a good catch, you could make an educated guess as to his location. Perhaps two hours ago you saw him heading SW and could figure approximately where he was from that. Many fishermen don't do that and haven't a clue where other boats are or who they are, and that is not good.

One day I saw a cute little Monterey boat chugging by with black smoke coming out of the exhaust and asked Ole who it was. He didn't know, but said he had often seen him around. I remained curious about the boat and some time later I was at Port Hueneme and there was the boat, tied up at the wharf. The name was ROSE MARIE and she was owned by Paul Helmick. A former owner was Ted "Tadpole" Runge of Santa Monica and he had built the cabin on the boat. A year or so later Paul retired and I bought the boat from him.

I was a brave young boy and having seen the boat at Guadalupe, I had no fear of going there myself. I would go anywhere the big boats went and when I was underway with a load of fish the stern was awash up to the fish hatch combing. I had to keep the cover on the trolling cockpit, but it didn't bother me. I figured if Paul could do it I could, too. The little ROSE MARIE rode like a duck and I never had a problem. Today I would be more cautious.

I was just outside Cortes Bank when the weather turned snotty and I stopped to use the sea anchor and ride it out. "Bicycle Howard" was with me and he was a little slow. I told him to pull in the jig lines as I got the drogue ready. I stopped the boat and, put out the sea anchor and backed down. The lines on one side were still out and four with their three-way swivels and jigs were caught on the propeller.

Howard asked, "What are we going to do?"

"Jump in and cut them out," was my answer.

When the boat settled on the anchor I went over the side, stood on the rudder and then dove under. The boat was pitching up and down six to eight feet in the swells and banged my head severely, but I got the lines cut and surfaced. Howard helped me get aboard and I was chilled and shaking. He was afraid I was going to die, but I got in my bunk and covered with all the blankets. Next morning I was okay and the weather moderated, so off we went in pursuit of the longfins.

Once when coming in from the Dumping Grounds with a load of albacore I was passing the East End of San Clemente Island. Cruising along in calm weather at 1,500 rpms on the 25 hp Cat diesel it seemed as if I was making good speed. In the distance I saw another boat overtaking and very soon it was closer and then it shot by like a rocket and was quickly out of sight toward Catalina. She was the LINDA, a beautiful Tacoma Boat Works 46-foot troller holding 16-18 tons. They usually cruise at eight knots loaded. I was puzzled and estimated that I was only making a disappointing five knots or less. It changed my whole outlook on boat speeds and as I was young and eager I wanted to go faster, but ROSE MARIE was churning along as fast as she could go.

Heading for the Showboat Spot on another trip, I had run a long way and stopped to rest. As it powered the refrigeration, I left the engine running and put the rudder hard over. When I woke up a few hours later, the engine sounded different. I found the boat going in circles. I saw three boats circling with me and knew they thought I was in trouble and were standing by to help. I went on deck and signaled that everything was okay. The Snow-Nabstedt gear box had slipped into gear and was stuck in forward. I didn't know how to fix it, so had to

Mike pumping bilge on HAPPY III. Fresh water barrel is atop bait tank.

Deckload of albacore on HAPPY III.

return to San Pedro and call Ed Velette, the Caterpillar mechanic, to show me how to adjust the clutch.

One of the most important things for a boat bait fishing for albacore is a tank of lively bait and lots of it. Knowing how to chum and make every piece of bait count is essential, especially if it is necessary to fish far offshore. Running inshore for live bait and back out can be costly in time, fuel and lost income. A good chummer can perhaps get a load of fish on one tank of bait when another may need two or three tanks of bait to get a load.

My first experience as an albacore chummer was on the HAPPY III. We had two Mexicans from Ensenada so the crew totaled four. I was the designated chummer. I knew how to chum on a sportboat, but this was entirely different. I became a good chummer by remembering the story of crewmen on the DONNA K.

Bernard Matara told of his one trip on the Kettenburg JOHN TRUE. They began with 60 scoops of bait and were fishing on the Dumping Grounds spot. Lots of stops were made for just a few albacore on each stop. Bernard was chumming all day and in the evening the skipper, Bob Carpenter, asked how much bait remained. "None," replied Bernard. Bob freaked out as they had only a ton of fish for that tank of bait. Bernard had never been on that kind of trip before, so to me it seemed Bob's fault for not noticing how much bait was being chummed away.

I have watched sportboats chumming albacore, brailing out scoops of bait on every stop. It was a good thing for them that they could get a full tank before their next trips. For commercial boats it is important that they be able to catch their own bait and not have to rely on someone else. It sometimes took hours or days of waiting before bait could be obtained. In the old days it took four or five men to haul a bait net by hand. If the net was small and conditions favorable, three men could pull it. A waiting boat would often put a man or two on a net boat to help.

Captains of net-equipped boats had different ways, some giving surplus bait to anyone who needed it, others giving only to their own special group. I liked to give bait to Stan Holloway on the SKIPALONG. He took only 20 scoops and his wife always rewarded us with a six-pack and a bag of tasty homemade cookies. On the CAROL JOAN in San Simeon Bay, we once gave away 400 scoops. The albacore were only eight or ten miles out so the first boats that baited up from us were out there catching a ton or more of fish while we were still handing out free bait. Mo on the FINITA took 160 scoops without a thank you. Our crew was wondering what the hell we were doing, wasting so much time being good guys.

Warren Beadle would give bait only to his special friends. If a boat came alongside for bait, but the skipper asked the fatal question, "How does it look, is it slimey?" We dumped the bait right under his nose. Sometimes they would attempt to scoop up what they could as it swam away. Warren preferred to catch his

Mike and wife Linda return from an albacore trip.

116

MARGIE, DOR-ANN and PATRICK between albacore trips.

bait at night while others were asleep and we would be hours ahead on the way to the fishing area.

That sort of albacore fishing is long past in California. The San Pedro and San Diego live bait albacore boats are all gone now. It was once a good way to make a buck, and I believe a small 10 or 15-ton bait boat could still make good local catches. There is only one problem: there are no more boats or people with knowhow to man them. Or there are no more who want to try it.

As for good catches of albacore on a small bait boat, the best was on the CAROL JO AN off of Monterey. Two of us caught 1,700 albacore in one day. We had other days of 700 to 800 a number of times, even on my own boat. One November off San Martin Island with Warren Beadle on the DOR-ANN we caught six tons of 27-pound average albacore in one stop. We could have caught more, but the entire deck was full up past the cabin so we had to stop. We were out of bait anyway.

Good Crewmen are Hard to Find

When I crewed on other boats I always tried to do my best and for my effort I was paid up to 25 percent of the catch. Now I needed two men on the

PIEFACE for live bait albacore fishing and found that good crews are hard to find.

In 1964 I fished live bait albacore all summer, from Cape Colnett to Monterey. I had one good crewman and needed another. A friend told me of a college student who had worked as deckhand for Dick Helgren on the REEL SPECIAL and now wanted to go commercial fishing. I got in touch and talked with him a little and decided he might be okay and off we went.

We were fishing around the 213 and 295 spots and he was the chummer, but did a half-assed job. I did the cooking and told him to hang on to his plate while

JO ANN MARIE making bait.

Three boats rigged for albacore live bait fishing. Warren Beadle's DOR-ANN in the center.

eating. When we shut down at day's end the boat drifts in the trough of the waves and sometimes rolls heavily. One night he didn't hang on and his plate of pork chops, green beans and applesauce went on the deck upside down. I saw it coming and it did. He said, "Captain, my food went on the floor. You will have to cook me some more." With that I yelled, "Scoop it up and eat it and shut up!" With a scared look he did as I said and ever after kept a grip on his plate.

We were working around a large fleet of commercial and sport boats and he spotted the REEL SPECIAL "There's Dick on the REEL. Can I call him on the radio and tell him I am on a commercial boat?" My answer was no, he was busy. He kept asking so finally I said okay, but I turned off the radio transmitter. He called and called and Dick never answered. "See, I told you he is really busy."

He kept falling asleep when he was supposed to be watching for jig strikes. It is important to see them the instant they bite so bait can be chummed to raise the school. Once I saw a strike and he was asleep. I waited

MONTALVO at the cannery pier.

TROJAN looking for albacore.

118

Doug Pate's CAROL JO AN at Monterey with a load of albacore squidded by Mike and Kenny Butler in one day of fishing.

awhile to give him a chance and then ran down and shook him.

"You were asleep!"

"Oh, no. I was just resting my eyes," he said.

"Pull the fish in now," I told him and advanced the engine to top speed. He cried for me to stop as the line was hurting his hands.

"Pull it in and stop being such a baby!" I roared. He complied and only fell asleep half as much after that.

He kept bugging me to get in the rack and "lift" some albacore, as he called it. I wouldn't let him, but finally gave him a chance. He decked his first fish all right and turned around in the rack and stuck the end of the pole right into the chummer's eye. Now we were in big trouble. The eye turned all red inside and I headed straight for port. Luckily for everyone, the eye was saved. Another boat owner, Russ Fernell, had just been sued for $100,000 for a similar accident.

Guess what? End of bozo's job on my boat.

HAPPY III

119

Tending seabass nets at the Channel Islands.

Mike tending the gillnet reel on Warren Beadle's boat.

Chapter 10
BARRACUDA AND WHITE SEABASS

After a few years I got interested in drift gillnet fishing for barracuda, but didn't know how. Based on experience, Warren Beadle gave me instructions and good advice. I bought some nets and tried my luck. I worked that fishery for 10 years and always made money, fishing from April to September. The nets were #6 nylon, 3 5/8 inch mesh, 165 meshes deep, 300-400 fathoms in length. They were suspended one and a half to two fathoms below the surface by buoys to allow boats to pass over them. Large ships and tugs with barges are the vessels fishermen dread.

Arriving at the chosen area about an hour before sunset, we looked for signs of fish: birds, bait and jumpers. The net was set just as the sun went down. The fish were usually on the surface at that time of day and cannot see the web as well as later when phosphorescence is "firing" in the pitch dark. After a couple of hours, the net is hauled back and the fish are picked on the way to port. At times an early morning set, just before dawn, is best, especially during a full moon.

When gillnet boats left port in the afternoon, they usually departed about the same time. Some came from Fish Harbor, some from Purse Seine Dock and some from the outer harbor. There were six or seven from San Pedro and four or five San Diego boats. If a boat made a good catch and the others did not know the location, they would follow and fish where he fished. One trick was to wait by the lighthouse and follow the successful boat, not from behind but just ahead, so he could not be accused of following.

Upon arriving at the chosen area the boat was slowed and a light buoy was launched. It was an inner tube supporting a piece of plywood with a lantern tied to it. No reliable battery lights were available then. The net was paid out as the boat cruised slowly ahead. The following boat would usually begin setting his net close by to block the first boat's gear from the fish as it drifted, usually to the eastward. When another boat tried this on me, I would put my buoy over and pay out the net very slowly for a short distance. The poacher would be making a fast set to block me. After 10 or 15 fathoms were out I would quickly pull it back and make a fast run to where I had really caught the fish. This would leave the follower in a spot where he might not catch anything and I would come in with a good load. The fish move and sometimes we both would be skunked.

Catch of barracuda on deck.

At the dock one day I saw two men talking to the crew of another Santa Barbara boat and sidled up to see who they were and what they wanted. They were from Ralph Story's L.A., a television documentary program. They wanted to film a fishing trip for the program, but the crew was reluctant and declined. I asked if they paid a fee and they said no because it was a documentary, but that there would be a free breakfast and dinner. I volunteered. "OK, we will be back at four P.M. to eat before we go out."

The director was Al Rosen, but I don't recall the name of the cameraman. Rosen said it would be a good idea to eat a fish dinner as it might bring good luck. I took them to Tony's café at 6th and Beacon in San Pedro. Rosen had salmon, the camera guy had halibut and I had shrimp. We got underway in the evening and at that time of day it is nearly always windy in the San Pedro channel. We had 15-18 knots of breeze as we rounded the lighthouse and choppy. Within minutes Rosen lost his salmon and by the time we got to the fishing grounds he was in bad shape. Al Rosen was a good sport, but I know he will never go out in a small boat again.

The net was set and with the end secured to the bow of the boat it acted as a sea anchor, holding the bow into the wind so she easily rode the swells. The TV guys filmed the entire process of setting the net and then plied me with questions. They shined a light in my face and asked about all kinds of things, such as: "Do fishermen get jealous when someone else catches fish and they don't?"

My answer, which I knew some fishermen would not like, was, "Yes, they do. I don't because if they catch fish it means I have a chance to get some too. If nobody catches any, then chances are not as good."

The day after the film was shown on TV I got a lot of abuse at the harbor. "What do you mean I get jealous?" Came from more than one fisherman, including a couple that surprised me, but you never know. Did it bother me? I considered the source.

At that time Los Angeles Harbor and even Catalina waters were very polluted by drill mud from oil well drilling in Long Beach Harbor. Every evening a barge would dump a load of drill mud at the Isthmus. Thousands of gallons of waste from the Proctor & Gamble soap plant in Wilmington were dumped in the water. It was something bad, yellow in color. There were no anchovies in the harbor then and if you took a tank of live bait into the harbor it would die on the spot. The barracuda would be migrating up or down the coast, but when they came in to the channel area they were gone in a flash.

Because of the poor water conditions, we didn't catch much when I took the TV crew. Al Rosen felt so bad that I hadn't caught much for all my effort to accommodate him that he gave me $100 in cash. Maybe I am the only person they ever paid.

Barracuda were for 50 years a major food fish and target species for both sport and commercial fishermen, Today they are a hard sell as people are eating farmed fish and don't like fish that taste like fish. When they are handled correctly, immediately bled and iced, the meat is snow white without a fishy taste. I still catch some in the summer by trolling and sell them. I offer them free or on a money-back deal if the buyer doesn't like them. Folks that get a free one return and buy again and those that paid never ask for their money back.

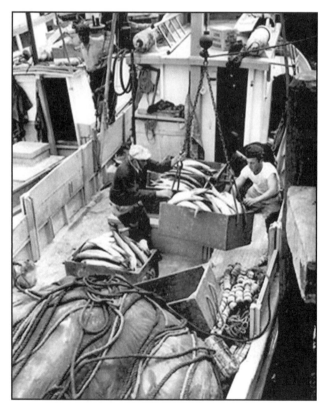
Boxing up a load of gillnet barracuda.

White Seabass

Gillnet fishing for white seabass was one of my favorite methods. Warren Beadle of Santa Monica first taught me how it was done. We fished the coast from the Point Sal to the Barn Kelp off San Onofre. In winter we fished at San Clemente Island and in El Nino years from Point Conception to Point Arguello. Winter fish prices were much higher than in summer as not many boats would brave the storms that could cause loss or damage to the nets. The gill nets are set alongside reefs or rocks and storm waves can cause the net anchors to drag and the nets to wash into the rocks.

We began fishing in Mexico from January to June and it was often a 72-hour run to the area. Sometimes, because of negative conditions, there were no fish to be had. In that case, it was necessary to search and it might take days to find the fish. The longest trips lasted up to 25 days.

With my boat PIEFACE I fished for seabass around the Channel Islands and on the coast from Point Dume to Point Conception for over 35 years. I would probably still be at it if it wasn't for Proposition 132 that prohibits gill net fishing within three miles of the coast and one mile of the islands. Those areas are where most of the seabass hang out.

White seabass are an interesting species, and if their peculiar habits are not learned, a fisherman will not do well. They move frequently according to moon phase, water temperature and food availability. They will show

Warren Beadle was the teacher of methods.

up when the weather is bad and the swells are huge, and in places that humans would consider unlikely.

Seabass are the favorite food of sea lions and harbor seals. There has been a population explosion of the animals in recent years. Even if fishing was allowed near the Channel Islands, it would now be nearly impossible to save any fish caught in a gill net. Seals wait by the net and immediately sense when a fish is hung. They swim down and eat the liver and guts first and move on to the next gilled fish.

Until the early 1960s sportfishermen caught lots of seabass, by day and night. A 20-year period of low daytime catches followed. I believe all old time sportboat captains retired and the new breed did not have the skill to catch them until they learned how to use live squid for bait. In the meantime, some anglers claimed that commercial fishermen were wiping out the resource.

Around the islands white seabass come in from deep water at night and in daylight return to the deep. If sportfishermen fish only in the daytime, the fish are often not present where he is, and if they are they bite only at certain times.

My nets were often set in kelp beds, floating the gear on the surface in Spring and Summer. The web hung down 15 or 20 feet from the surface and it caught very few fish other than seabass: a few leopard sharks and an occasional sheephead or yellowtail. When sports cast jigs at my boat, my son Dana would ask, "Why do

Dana McCorkle admires a dandy white seabass.

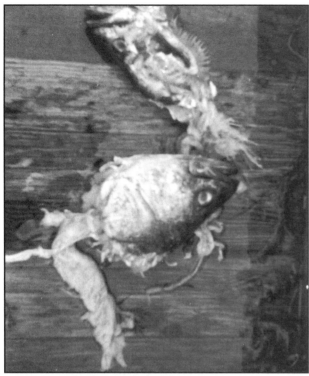

Seabass mutilated by sea lions.

they do that? We don't even catch what they do." All I could answer is that they were uninformed about how we fished and don't ever bother to find out.

Occasionally one or two San Pedro boats would show up at the Channel Islands. Some knew where to fish, and some did not. They were all used to fishing in the same places near San Pedro: Portuguese Bend, Horseshoe Kelp, Dago Bank, Huntington Flats, etc. Boats unfamiliar with the islands would look for the local boats and set their gear right alongside of them.

One boat cruised into China Bay on Santa Cruz Island and checked me out. My nets were a short 65-70 fathoms long, anchored at each end. To pull the net, I started at one end, picking up the anchor and bringing the net aboard. The fish, if any, were removed as the net came in. When the end of the net was reached, the anchor was either hauled and a move was made, or if some fish were caught, it was let back out, leaving the anchor in place. When the net is reset, the first anchor and its marker buoy are dropped.

The Pedro boat watched us pull and saw us pick some fish. When we were at the far end of our net he moved in front of us and began setting his net right in our spot. He thought we could not set back as he had taken the spot, an old San Pedro trick. Having grown up there, I was aware of those moves and set my net back right over the top of his. The way I saw it, my net was not out of the water when he set, so it was still my spot.

The intruder could not pull his net because it was under mine. He yelled and complained, but it did him no good. After an exchange of words, we went on about our business. Next morning when we pulled he was watching to make sure we did not cut his net. We caught a few and he caught none. He never tried that trick on me again. If you do not make a stand as we did, poachers will run you out of your own fishing grounds. That is the way it goes in the fishing jungle.

I have seen crazy behavior over a few fish. Guns were pulled and threats made, but not much shooting. Sometimes the first to pull a gun ends up looking down the barrel of the other boat's gun and hears, "Start shooting, mother------!" I've seen similar confrontations while harpooning swordfish.

In the '60s I did a lot of gillnet fishing for white seabass in the kelp beds from Pt. Conception to Santa Barbara. In April I would begin just below Gaviota Pier and fish down to Coal Oil Point. The nets were floated on the surface in the middle of the kelp and would hang down about 15 feet. Each end was anchored and flagged so boats would not run over the corkline and cut it.

To run the net I used a 16-foot skiff after tying my boat to one end of the net. Passing along the net I removed the fish and did not have to pull the whole net out of the kelp every day. There were certain spots seabass seemed to favor and I learned the landmarks for them.

At the time the kelp beds were huge and thick. I would run my boat in and out from the shore to cut a lane where I could set my net so that it would hang correctly.

The Kelco Company in San Diego would send their cutters to harvest the kelp where I fished. The skippers

Mike's son Dana fished with his dad.

124

were good guys who would cut channels through the weeds where I could set my nets. The kelp grew back in a matter of days.

Kelco had four cutter barges: the older EL WOOD and EL REY and the new steel boats KELMAR and KELSOL. One day the EL WOOD broadcast a May-day signal that she was loaded and sinking near Coal Oil Point. I was on my way north to Pt. Conception and was in the area in an hour or so. There was a lot of loose kelp in the water and a skiff and the Coast Guard searched until dark, but no survivors were found. A deckhand's body was discovered in the kelp at Gaviota a couple of days later and a week or so later the captain's corpse was found on the beach at Morro Bay.

As we trawled for shrimp and cucumbers in the area we were concerned that we might snag the wreck of the kelp cutter. A number of years passed without trouble before the large trawler GUS D. caught something very heavy and towed it along the bottom to Goleta Beach and dropped it near the sewer outfall. The captain told Shane Anderson of the UCSB lab about it. Divers went down and reported a large flat-bottomed, twin screw, barge-like vessel which turned out to be the EL WOOD. The hulk is still there today and is a haven for lobsters.

The KEL SOL, newest of the kelp cutters, was working between Goleta Point and Coal Oil when she capsized and was floating bottom-up when I passed by. I heard they had ballasting problems. I was sad to see the rudder, keel and propellers sticking out of the water. The boat had a conventional cutwater bow for cruising and the cutters were in the stern so that she went backwards when chopping kelp. She was salvaged and eventually resumed her work.

The great storms of 1982 tore up all the kelp beds from Gaviota to Santa Barbara. The root base that had formed there over many years was destroyed and covered with sand. According to the kelp company biologists, there may never be kelp growing there in our lifetime. I was lucky to have fished there in "the good old days."

PIEFACE at Santa Barbara, ready for gillnetting or swordfishing.

Ready for weigh-in and delivery.

Pulling a seabass gillnet on AMELIA, 1929.

Mike patching a net.

THERESA ANNE ready for salmon trolling.

Baiting lines for rockfish.

Chapter 11
OTHER FISHERIES

Rock Cod Fishing

In the old days I did quite a lot of hook-and-line rock cod fishing. A Raytheon 721B paper meter on my Monterey ROSE MARIE was a good tool for finding fish. I worked around the West End of Catalina and the South Bank off Redondo. There was no loran, radar or GPS, so a person had to go by depth, landmarks and navigation charts to locate the productive areas. If today's sports had to do it that way it would be tough for them to catch fish.

After moving to Santa Barbara in 1964, I found some of the local fishermen working an area they called the "12-mile Reef" in the middle of the channel between SB and Santa Cruz Island, 12 miles south of the harbor. When fishing was slow for other species, they would go for rockfish. It was a good spot with reds, chuckleheads, bocaccio and chilipeppers, I figured it would be good around the islands of Santa Rosa and San Miguel, but I found that the wind blows most of the time there and a lot of time was spent riding at anchor waiting for fishable weather.

The Finger Bank was just inside the wind much of the time and more fishing could be done. There I met a couple of expert fishermen that showed me a couple of

good spots and how to fish with a large array of hooks. Mitch Ruda from Avila Beach was one, and Red Allen on the VINCENT K. was the other.

Using squid or salted anchovies, I would bait up 1,000 hooks, 50 hooks on a ganglion. I had the lines coiled in flat boxes with an open end. Three 50–hook ganglions would often be connected and could bring up 150 fish at a time. The type of fish biting could be determined from the way they pulled on the line.

Pat Brofie on the KITRIE and I were fishing on the Finger one day and using two or three lines buoyed off so we could rotate pulling them. I saw a party boat approaching and picked up my lines and moved slowly off the bank so he wouldn't see exactly where I was fishing. Pat kept fishing and the boat STAR ANGLER, Capt. John Worobief, came up and made a couple of slow circles around Pat and then went on his way toward Oxnard. Ten minutes later he called another boat on his radio and said, "I think I have found a new area. There is a couple of commercial boats here and I see fish. I'll be out tomorrow and check it out." As they did not know about the spot, not one party boat had been seen there before. He came back the next day and caught limits. That was the end of commercial catches there.

On weekends there would be eight to ten sportboats

fishing with live anchovies and light monofilament line. When that kind of gear has been used, it is the only thing the fish will bite on. We had been using cotton or nylon handlines and dead bait. Funny how that happens, but it does. The sports eventually had to go to 30-pound test mono to get fish. We just quit going out there.

John bought the 85-foot RED ROOSTER in San Diego and renamed it RANGER 85. He fished San Miguel consistently and caught 250 tons of rockfish out there. A good commercial boat caught about 100 tons.

The last time I fished on the Finger I was at the harbor when some guys decided to go to the Finger for some rock cod to eat. We went with nylon lines and squid for bait. It was the weekend and there were lots of sports around. We found some fish and dropped on them. No bites. A number of spots were tried with the same result. The NEW DINAH LEE was drifting near us and doing well so we moved over and drifted on his fish. Not a nibble. The NEW DINAH LEE folks were now angry at us. I suggested we run up-current from him and we picked up some small floaters they were throwing back and went home.

Once I left a buoy on a big spot of chilipeppers when I quit after a successful day of fishing. I had taken about 1,500 pounds and there were plenty left. I never left a marker that way before but there was no one around and I figured it would be safe. I would be back

NEW DINA LEE did well with rock cod.

at dawn the next morning. I overslept and as I was leaving the harbor I heard on the radio John Worobief saying, "I just found this buoy and its loaded." I thought, "There goes my fish!" When I got there the STAR ANGLER was 75-80 yards away from the buoy and reporting to his friends, "Limits on one short drift." I ran updrift from him to the buoy and metered fish scattered all along the bottom. I picked up the buoy and left, telling myself I had been really stupid.

Gillnet fishing for rockfish was a big deal at Monterey for a time, so I made 80 nets so I could fish in my area. The first time out we set the nets near a rockpile in 35 fathoms. The net must be close beside the rocks, but not right on them as the net will snag and be torn to pieces. After an overnight soak, we pulled the nets the next morning and they were full of ratfish (monkey sharks) and dogfish sharks. All the sharks and the few rockfish in the net had been eaten by slime eels. Mud bottoms are full of the obnoxious creatures which eat their way inside a fish and leave nothing but a bag of skin.

To avoid the slime eels the nets were moved to another spot with a harder bottom. Good fish marks made us hopeful and the next morning when we began pulling, up came 200 pounds of mixed rockfish in the first 100 feet if net. We thought, "Oh boy, we are gonna do okay!" The net was getting heavy, but I figured when the fish came up they would pop their swim bladders and float the net.

The weight turned out to be a 40-foot basking shark that had twisted and rolled the rest of the net around its body like a cocoon. Basking sharks have very rough skin with a slime that chafes a net until it comes apart. It was the end of a brand-new net and the end of rock-code gillnetting for me. It really didn't bother me a bit.

Sportboat angler with a catch of chilipeppers.

Mike Taormina's COQUETTA.

Red Allen and I built a large fish trap with the idea of making big catches and big money on the Finger Bank. The trap was 4x6 feet, almost a the size of a king crab pot, and would hold a lot of fish. With high hopes we baited the trap with anchovies, squid and abalone guts and put it on a nice area of chuckleheads. We fished with hook-and-line while waiting for the trap to fill up. We were getting 25 hooks full on each drop and were stoked. Using a winch, we began pulling the heavy trap. In 85 fathoms it took a while, but after it got close to the surface the fish would float it, perhaps coming up under the boat and punching a hole in it. When it surfaced, there was not one fish in it! We tried it once more, and still no fish, and we gave up on the trap fishing. I know now it would have worked with the proper trap funnel for the fish to enter. It was another idea that didn't pan out. I have tried many in my life; some worked and some didn't, but you don't know if you don't try.

From every port along the coast there once was a large number of boats fishing with hook-and-line for rockfish. A few worked all year, but most fished from November to June. In warm summer water blue sharks

Overhauling rockfish lines.

are abundant and can destroy fishing gear in a few short hours. The only way to prevent it is to pull the lines quickly and get the fish out of the water. It is difficult if there are a large number of fish on the line.

In San Diego the FOUR BROTHERS used to tie up at the second finger pier by Kettenburg Boat Works and put up a long pole with a red flag. People in the neighborhood would see the signal and come to the boat and buy part of his catch. The owner was Frank Passanisi and I think he was one of the best rock cod fishermen in San Diego. FOUR BROTHERS was a nice Monterey boat with a gas engine, later powered by a GM 2-71. Frank sold the boat and went back to the Old Country where he came from as a youngster. The boat was later hit by a ship and sunk.

A half-dozen boats from San Pedro fished every winter, making trips of two weeks or more. On lengthy trips boats had to lie at anchor waiting for the weather to moderate. They worked around Santa Rosa, San Miguel and San Nicholas Islands and on the Tanner, Cortes and 70-90 Banks. One boat I know of, CALI- FORNIA REPUBLIC, was on her anchor for at San Miguel for 17 days before the weather calmed, but she loaded up in two days.

My friend "Dago Mike" Taormina on the COQUETTA anchored for eight days at Johnson's Lee, Santa Rosa, waiting for other boats to leave so he could go to his secret hot spot. On a foggy day he was fishing on the southwest edge of the Santa Rosa Flats when he heard engine noise. Out of the fog came the RANGER 85 and skipper John Worobief, who yelled from the pilot house, "Don't worry, Mike. I won't tell anyone!" He did not realize the effect live bait and monofilament gangions would have on that spot.

Mike always kept two barrels full of salted bait on his boat. Barracuda and bonito were his favorites and we often gave him shorts to fillet for the salt tubs. He fished hook-and-line rock cod for 60 years and quit only because of his age. One April day he was heading for San Pedro from Santa Rosa, passing Anacapa Island on the weather side. He spotted a swordfish and har- pooned it and six others and delivered the fish at Santa Barbara. It was a very unusual occurrence. We had taken swordfish around Anacapa in May, but never that early in the year.

There were eight wholesale fish dealers in San Pedro that bought most of the rock cod. Some boats sold all their catch to one market; others sold a box or two to different dealers. The markets were very com- petitive and preferred to get the whole catch so they could sell to the competitors. Boats with poor quality fish would get less money per pound than those that brought in high quality catches. "Jewfish Louie Zermattan" was known for not-so-high quality. "Dago Mike" always had good quality and usually got more money for his fish. I once asked him which was his favorite rock cod for eating and he liked bocaccio. He brought in all varieties: reds, cows, chilies, chuckleheads, bocaccios, etc. Reds (vermilion rockfish) were often the largest part of the catch and were favorites of the public.

Today no rock cod boats are selling to those markets. The few boats still fishing sell in downtown Los Angeles where they get top prices. The San Pedro dealers pay high prices for Canadian filleted fish, but will not pay a local boat the same price. Beside COQUETTA and CALIFORNIA REPUBLIC, other regular rock-codders where LUMINA, CALIFORNIA GIRL, LIDA B. II, VISIT, ADVENTURA and EAGLE. were also some small boats making day trips in their local waters.

One year the 50-foot ex-trawler GRACE H. from Morro Bay anchored in Johnson's Lee at Santa Rosa, Using a beam trawl, she was the boat that pioneered the pink shrimp fishery in Morro Bay. The owner was a black man, unusual in California fisheries. I was trapping lobsters with Danny Mack and we had some gear near the Lee. The owner of the GRACE H. hailed us, waved us over and asked if we had any "red rabbits" he could buy. We wondered what he meant and he said, "The things you are taking out of those cages."

We gave him some babies and he invited us aboard for coffee and cake. His sweet wife was a good housekeeper and had put clean white sheets on their bunks, a luxury not often seen on commercial fishing boats. Every time we met up afterward we dropped off a few "red rabbits" and enjoyed a good snack. When I asked how he was doing with rock cod and he would say, "Yesterday we got a ton." Later I was told that when he unloaded in San Pedro he usually had less than 1,000 pounds, To this day I still call lobsters "red rabbits."

It is too bad we can't fish for rockfish as we did in those days. The fish are still out there, but in my lifetime I don't see ever being able to catch enough to make it worthwhile. Too many restrictions and area closures.

Bait Merchant

Among the ways I tried to earn a living for a few years was selling live bait through an independent receiver in Santa Barbara Harbor. I got half the money. As soon as I delivered bait to the receiver, harbor seals would rip open the webbing walls of the wells and the bait would go bye-bye. I tried selling bait off my boat

Mike the bait merchant

anchored at the harbor entrance. The sport fishermen didn't know it was allowed and passed me up, even though a sign was up and I was yelling at them. I told the receiver owner that he needed to make seal-proof wells, but he didn't want to spend the money. I ceased bringing bait to him and found other outlets. At times I ran the 60 miles to Redondo to find bait and when the sportfishing landing ran out, I had the only bait in town.

Sometimes I trawled and caught bait on the same day. We built a tank that fit inside the hatch combing; six feet deep with sides four by three and a half feet. I kept the bait net in the tank while trawling for halibut, came in to unload the catch and off-load the halibut net doors on the dock.

The lampara bait net would be pulled out of the tank and used to surround the bait fish. I would haul the net on my gillnet reel which I used for trawling at the same time. Sometimes I went out by myself and would run the boat from the stern controls while I dumped the bag, ran to the bridge to complete the circle and picked up the keg buoy. If I missed the keg, I was in deep trouble, but I learned to do it night or day.

There are two methods for hauling a lampara net with a gillnet reel. One way is to pull both wings over the reel. Two men are needed and the bag must be pulled all

130

Mike and the gurdies that spool the wire trolling lines.

the way over the reel to be restacked. With a drum winch the net can be taken off the side of the drum anytime. With the second method both wings of the net are wound on the reel. It is very important to keep the wings even and colored floats on the corklines tell if one wing is ahead of the other. They can be adjusted by moving higher or lower on the reel as it turns. The bag has to come over the top of the reel to be restacked. A variation is to stack one wing as it comes in , but the other wing must be unwound and pulled behind the boat to stretch it out for restacking. This can be done by two men, or even one, but it is slow and laborious for one man. The advantage of using a powered reel is it is possible for one person to haul the net. The owner of ANTOINETTE W. at Oceanside still pulls his net by this method.

I began selling salted bait to Lou Ferrari in San Francisco for use on his rock cod lines. He bought a ton of salted anchovies a week. I would haul up two tons at a time and sell the rest to other fishermen. If Louie bought it, they also had to have it. They were Italians, Sicilians, and some people have a hard time doing business with them. Not me. I grew up fishing among them and it was not a problem.

Lou was a top high-liner and the first to buy bait from me so he got all he wanted. His 80-year-old uncle had fished for rock cod over 50 yeas in a 30-foot Monterey with only a compass for navigation. He was the bait inspector for each delivery. He would meet me and he would take a handful of it, feel it, eyeball it, and give the OK. The other fishermen would stand around and watch. On his first trip to Cordell Bank using my bait Lou caught a little over four tons in one day. He

sold in China Town for a much better price than the markets paid.

I had three other steady customers and we got along just fine. One day a guy who had I had seen around, but had never bought before, approached me to buy bait. I gave him a price of 20 cents a pound or $50 a barrel (about 250 pounds) and he agreed to buy some. To cure and preserve the bait fish there is about 85 pounds of salt in each barrel. With both hands he began taking bait from my barrel, washing off the salt, and putting only the fish in his barrel.

I knew at once what he was up to and had to figure out how to keep from being swindled. A bystander told me, "John is smart like a fox." I had to agree. When he had transferred all the bait, only salt and brine were left in my barrel. He weighed the fish and they came to around 150 pounds. He paid the fish only price, with no salt or brine. Then he asked for some of the juice and I replied with $1 a pound price. He didn't want to pay, so he had the bait with no juice. The fish were fresh and needed a little more time to cure, but without the salt and brine they spoiled in a few days. The next week I was back and the fishermen came and picked up their bait. John also asked for more, but I told him, "Sorry, looks like I don't have any for you. It's all gone." Smart like a fox he was not.

After a few years I lost my market. A local boat began supplying salt bait at Fisherman's Wharf and for me it no longer paid. I never made much money at it, but enjoyed doing it. Every time I see Louie he tells me my bait was the best he ever bought from anyone, and that makes me feel good.

A Monterey trolling for salmon.

Salmon Troller

For salmon trolling I have two boats with California salmon permits: PIEFACE, 35 feet and THERESA ANNE, 30-foot Monterey. Both boats can fish salmon, but since 1996 I have used only THERESA ANNE. If there are no salmon in the area I fish (Pt. Arguello to Dana Point) I can target other species with PIEFACE.

In the mid-'60s I knew little about salmon trolling, but as a director of the Pacific Coast Federation of Fishermen's Associations, I met many salmon fishermen and listened to their conversations. In July, August and September, salmon were being caught in deep water seabass gillnets from Dana Point to Newport Beach. We were told the fish came from Irvine Creek and were returning there to spawn. This sounded logical, but I soon learned Irvine Creek was a mudhole and the fish were from the Sacramento River system.

When I moved to Santa Barbara a few boats were trolling for salmon in season. I went out with Billy Meng in his 29-foot Monterey, the SMK. He was an old friend from our San Pedro days when we fished together for barracuda. He had hydraulic gurdies fitted on his boat and we caught some salmon. Excited by our catch, I bought two hand-crank gurdies, collected a lot of king salmon knowhow from old timer Don Stairs and shop talk in *Fishermen's News* magazine and off I went. The fish were often in 30-40 fathoms, so it took a lot of cranking to bring them in. After a few years of trial and error I figured out how to catch a few. My best day was in 1982 when I took 126 salmon averaging 14 pounds from 6 am to 1 P.M. I had other good days of 50-75 fish. I was now ready to buy hydraulic gurdies and make some really big catches. I traded a sailboat for some two-spool gurdies and was able to use four lines instead of two. Looking back, many times I did just as well or better with the two lines.

In the old days salmon trollers used cotton or hemp lines pulled by hand. One to four pound weights were attached to the line at intervals and could total up to 40 pounds. That is a lot of weight to pull by hand from a moving boat, especially when there is a big fighting salmon on the end. Small, hand-cranked winches, called gurdies, were invented to ease the task and eventually powered hydraulic gurdies became standard. Modern gurdies are spooled with stainless wire line 1/16 or 5/64 inches in diameter. Fishing at depths of 100 fathoms is possible using 60 pound cannonball sinkers. Leaders are attached to the nearly vertical wire line with snaps at 1/2 to 3 fathom intervals marked by brass stops swaged to the line.

Salmon do not migrate below Point Conception every year, but at times they go all the way to Cape San Lucas, About every 10 years we have a nice run, every five years an okay run, The three years, 2004-07, were very poor. The northern boats that come down here to fish have a hard time as they are used to dirty, cold water, which isn't usual down here. Sometimes the water is clear blue with 25-30 feet of visibility and the salmon bite like crazy. The northerners leave 40-50 fish a day to go back and fish in brown water, 25 knots of wind and air temperatures in the high 40s, for 1-20 fish a day. I have caught salmon off Newport Beach in 73-degree surface temperature water. Sports trolling around for bonito, barracuda and mackerel would come alongside and ask what I was catching. When I said, "Salmon" they said "BS." Then I would hold up a nice 20-pounder and tell them the fish were down 180 feet. They couldn't believe it.

Commercial salmon trollers are like many sports;

A load of cucumbers in the cod end of the trawl net.

buying and trying all kinds of lures in search of the ultimate "Weapon of Mass Destruction" that will catch more and bigger fish. They buy different colors and patterns of hoochies, spoons, flashers and plugs and it can be frustrating and expensive. Sometimes only one hoochie will work and maybe a week later a different one is hot, and the first won't catch another fish for years. There are a few good standard lures that seem to work consistently, but something new will sometimes be a deadly killer.

Over the years the boats have begun trolling faster and early in the season using all flasher-hoochie combos. Later they turn to bait and are cruising along faster than they did 10 years ago. Wild king salmon are one of the most beautiful fish in the ocean, with excellent eyesight and very powerful bodies. If they don't want to come on your boat, there is a good chance you won't land them.

Sea cucumbers ready for processing.

Shrimp and Cukes

As one who was always trying new methods for catching under-utilized fish, I was responsible for creating several new fisheries. After obtaining an X Permit I had to test the new gear for a year before it was approved or disapproved by the Dept. of Fish & Game.

One development was a special large-mesh gillnet for angel sharks. They were plentiful and taken incidentally with gillnets and trammel nets set for other fish. In some summers I fished for halibut at San Miguel Island and they were abundant there. No one believed the sharks were edible except Italians and Slavs who knew them as food fish in the Old Countries. Also fishing at the island was a Slav gillnetter from San Pedro who told me how they caught them in Europe. We built some nets with large mesh, only a few meshes deep, modifying and improving them as we went along and they worked well. A whole new fishery commenced and certain seafood restaurants used the angel shark meat exclusively for fish and chips meals. Proposition 132 closed the areas of shark abundance and killed the fishery.

In the Santa Barbara Channel lives the ridgeback shrimp, a species once un-utilized, as no one knew how to catch them. Long ago, when fishing for white seabass in Mexico with Warren Beadle, I watched the Mexican double-rigged shrimp boats and the memory helped me figure out a way to tow a net using my gillnet reel. I purchased a small shrimp net and some spreader doors form Marinovich Trawl in Biloxi and set out to teach myself how to fish for shrimp. Next, I had to get an X Permit, figure out where the shrimp were most plentiful, and find a place to sell them. We had a Fishermen's Association market at Santa Barbara harbor and we began selling them there. I received 50 cents a pound

and they were retailed for $1 a pound. The public loved them and the fishery was viable. It is still a good fishery after 30 years, but is now under pressure from United Anglers and environmentalists who want to kill it.

A few years after we began fishing for ridgeback shrimp I took a Fish & Game biologist out to study the impact of sea lions on the shrimp trawl nets. He saw cucumbers in my net and mentioned there was a buyer for them in San Pedro. I was shocked as I couldn't imagine what they would do with them. "Eat them,"said the biologist.

A few weeks later, I was eating breakfast at Connetti's restaurant near the San Pedro markets when he came in with news that there were boats unloading cucumbers at the pier. I went for a look and found they were different from the few I caught. I got the buyers name and number and gave him a call and he said he would buy the kind I caught and to "Go and get me some."

I managed to make a catch and called Mr. Mu, who said, "Yeah, yeah," he would be up to get them. He never showed and the cucumbers melted. When he finally arrived, the quality was no longer satisfactory. I had to determine a method to keep them happy so they wouldn't melt. I designed a net that catches only cucumbers and was able to bring in a high quality product.

I discovered the cucumbers migrate inshore and out at different times of the year and found where they live between Point Conception and San Diego, the time of year they are in the best condition in each area, and where they are most abundant at different times of the year. In the Fall sea cucumbers are thick-walled and spit out their insides to grow new ones. In the Spring they are thin-walled and spawning, but the changes vary along the coast. From what I have seen, I think it has to do with water temperatures.

133

Halibut in the cod end of the trawl net.

Mike with a live halibut.

There was a better market for trawled cucumbers than the warty sea cucumbers the divers brought in. Mr. Mu wanted to set up business in Santa Barbara. I found him a spot in the fish market area and he opened a shop in which he dries the cukes. He has now been there for 30 years.

Once again I had to get an X Permit to start the fishery. Other fishermen scoffed and said I was crazy for trying. After I figured out how and where to catch them, they too began fishing for them. It is a good fishery and after a year or so of experimentation was approved by the Fish & Game. There is now a limited entry for cucumbers, diving or trawling, but the demand is steady. By taking care of the resource we have a small but sustainable and profitable fishery.

Live Halibut

A new fishery was established in the early 1970s when an area was opened for halibut trawling one to three miles offshore from Point Arguello to Point Mugu. There was a seasonal closure from March 15th to June 16th to protect spawners. An X Permit was also required. Halibut trawl gear is the only type with these restrictions. A large 7.5-inch mesh cod end is mandatory to allow the escape of small fish. Outside three miles the legal mesh is 4.5 inches. A Fish & Game observer went out on the Castagnola boat CECELIA for one year

Ready to set the cod end of the trawl net.

Light-Touch Artisanal Modified Paranzella Trawl Net

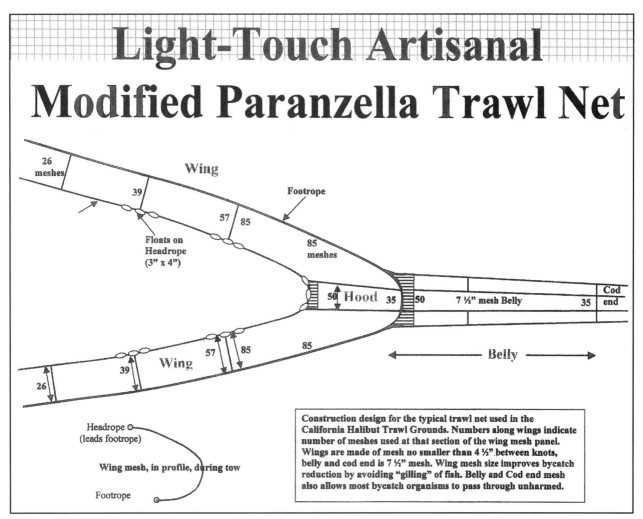

Construction design for the typical trawl net used in the California Halibut Trawl Grounds. Numbers along wings indicate number of meshes used at that section of the wing mesh panel. Wings are made of mesh no smaller than 4 ½" between knots, belly and cod end is 7 ½" mesh. Wing mesh size improves bycatch reduction by avoiding "gilling" of fish. Belly and Cod end mesh also allows most bycatch organisms to pass through unharmed.

Typical trawl net diagram. The halibut net has an escape aperture for undersize fish.

and determined that this was a good, clean fishery and should be allowed and it has flourished ever since. About 10 years ago a market developed for live halibut at double the price. At this time United Anglers is trying to eliminate this fishery and has made all sorts of false claims about it.

The new Ocean Protection Council, which will be controlling many fisheries in the future, is searching for new low volume-high value fishing methods. People are busy scrambling for grant money to determine what they could be. We already have three that fit the requirements: live halibut, live ridgeback shrimp, and sea cucumbers. Instead of giving us credit for the research work we have already done, some folks are trying to shut us down.

Fishing can be a dangerous business.

Mike's multipurpose PIEFACE, successful in eight fisheries: albacore, swordfish, rockfish, bait fish, white seabass, sea cucumbers, ridgeback shrimp, live halibut.

Mike McCorkle is a fighter for fishermen's rights to make a living from the sea.

Chapter 12
PERILOUS PROFESSION

Albacore Close Calls

Fishing on the high seas has its share of danger and I have had some close calls. On the WINIFRED II we were albacore fishing when the weather blew up and we ran for Morro Bay. The wind and swell increased all day and by the time we got in it was very rough. We heard other boats on the radio that were running for shelter also, some to San Simeon, some to Morro Bay and some to Avila Beach. A Newport Beach boat, the MARTHA JUNE, was heading for Morro Bay. I knew the owner, Vern, who had three Mexicans aboard as crew. The boat had been built by the same yard as my PIEFACE, but she had a hard chine and a transom stern. The previous owner, Gene Hachez, traded Vern for a different type of boat he wanted for soupfin shark fishing.

MARTHA JUNE never showed up in Morro Bay and I supposed Vern had gone to San Simeon or Avila. The wind blew for four or five days and I grew anxious about him and radioed boats at the other ports, but no one had seen Vern. I called his wife in Newport and she said he was fishing off Morro Bay.

She asked, "Is anything wrong?"

I said, "No," but knew different. A week later the boat's bait tank was found floating off San Miguel Island.

No other trace of the MARTHA JUNE or her people were ever found. It was before e-pirbs and inflatable rafts were carried to ensure a better chance of surviving a disaster.

On the PIEFACE in 1964 we were fishing for albacore with live bait outside San Simeon. It had been foggy for a week and at night, because it was safer than drifting, I would go in and anchor in the bay. The fish were fairly close in, so we didn't lose too much fishing time. I had a compass, radio direction finder, and an AM radio, but no radar, so getting in wasn't too much fun. The visibility was usually around 200 feet

We ran out at daylight and sometimes you could see a mile, for a few minutes. I lowered one jig pole and line and had another line off the stern while trolling for a jig-strike. Although visibility was zero, a few fish were biting and we got stopped. I was in the rack when all of a sudden out of the fog came the WARRIOR, a big 90-foot trawler-troller, her rudder hard over, turning as she passed down our side about 30 feet away. If we had collided she would have cut through us like butter. WARRIOR had passed on the side where our jig pole was housed upright or we would have lost it. I decided not to move until we had some visibility. Presently the fog lifted slightly for about 100 yards and there was the WARRIOR, also wisely stopped.

A nice troll-caught Santa Barbara salmon.

Few boats had radar in those days and it is amazing that there were not more collisions.

A couple of weeks later we were working outside Monterey where there were a lot of bird schools over the fish. Boats were running from one school to another. Several medium-sized San Diego bait boats were there: MARIE LOUISE, LONE WOLF, SOUTH SEAS, JULIA B, VENETIAN, SHASTA. All were chasing jumpers and bird schools. I spotted a nice school about 50 yards away and headed for them. The MARGARET F., a 75-foot ex-sardine seiner, saw them also. I was closer and got on the fish. I jumped in the rack and caught 25 or 30 fish real fast. I looked up and the ex-seiner was coming right at us. The boat had a top pilothouse with a flying bridge outside it. A Mexican crewman was on the bridge and the captain was inside the house steering the boat and taking directions from the man outside who was pointing at the fish breaking off our stern. I don't think the captain saw us and was going to run us down. I ran up and kicked our boat ahead fast and just in time. The MARGARET F. passed about 30 feet astern.

I wasn't sure if he did that on purpose as they were chumming heavily and the men were in the racks.

Some big boats do stuff like that to little boats. I left feeling that any minute he would be cussing me out for being in his way, even though I had beaten him to the fish. He didn't get too many fish out of the school anyway as all the churning around spooked them. Soon he called me on the radio and apologized, said he didn't see me. I felt better about the incident, but still if I hadn't looked up in time he would have sunk me. If you are on a little boat it is better not to get yourself in that kind of situation.

He Opened the Wrong Valve

In the mid '60s I sometimes would tie up my boat and go with Warren Beadle on the DOR-ANN from January to May fishing in Mexico for white seabass. We fished mostly from Abreojos to just above Magdalena Bay. On one trip fish were scarce as the water was cold, but we found a few on the Santa Domingo Bank. We had been there a couple of days and were about to move, but decided we would try it one more day. The bank is about eight or ten miles offshore and we would anchor there at night. When the weather was breezy it was not a lot of fun.

In the morning when we were pulling the net, along came a 58-foot bait boat from San Pedro, the SHOSHONE. She pulled up alongside and her owner Wally Hughes told us he was heading to the beach to look for bait. We gave him a couple of seabass to eat and off he went in search if bait. While he was alongside, I noticed that the lower cabin had only one small window on each side where the galley was and just one door on the after right side of the deckhouse. To me it seemed that it would be difficult to get out in an emergency.

That day we caught about 50 fish, and as reports from other boats up and down the coast were poor, we

MARTHA JUNE was lost with all hands.

reset the nets. After the set we were stowing the fish in the hold when I looked inshore and noticed something odd heading toward us with a waving flag.

I alerted Beadle and we watched as a small boat approached. As it got closer we could see it was Wally and his crew in their bait skiff and one was waving an oar with a T-shirt attached. The men were covered with diesel oil and the cover for the outboard motor was off and filled with diesel-soaked oranges.

Wally explained that they had caught some bait and had the net alongside ready to transfer the bait to the tanks. Wally had gone below to open valves to fill the wells and tanks with water and had mistakenly turned on the valve that put water for the spray brine system into the hatch. No large volume of water is needed for the spray system and if not turned off it will quickly flood the hatch hold.

The boat also had two wells filled with spare diesel fuel and as the bait was being scooped aboard the boat began to roll heavily. Wally ran below to see what was happening and discovered the open spray valve and closed it. It was too late and the water in the main hold shifted and the boat rolled onto its side. Wally made a dash for the back door, but the incoming water pushed him back into the cabin. The crew climbed on the side of the cabin and could see Wally through the small galley window. They broke the window out with the butt of a bait pole, and although Wally was bigger than the opening, they pulled him through after a struggle that severely scraped his hide.

The spare fuel in the wells spilled as the boat went down and the crew was covered with it. After we got them aboard I suggested they get rid of the oil oranges, but the crew declined as they "might need them." It was an indication of the effect of the disaster and close call they had just experienced. They were lucky we had set our nets back or we would have been gone. We were the only boat for miles around and eight miles away at that. If they had gone to the beach it is unlikely they would have made it through the high surf in that area.

Beadle cruised the DOR-ANN to where the SHOSHONE was floating bottom up. Wally said he had $5,000 in a box in the top cabin and he would give me $1,000 if I dove down and got the box. I said, "No, thank you." Maybe I would have done it 15 years earlier.

We made radio contact with Bill Horner on the tuna seiner BEVERLY LYNN, coming up the coast about 15 miles out, and ran out to meet him. Wally and his crew were transferred and taken to San Pedro. Another lucky break for them.

Wally rented an oil supply boat from Santa Bar-

Mike with a nice trawled halibut that will provide many fish dinners for happy customers.

bara and sent it south to make a salvage effort while he went looking for the SHOSHONE with an airplane. He found it in the same area with the stern still floating, but when the salvage boat arrived Shoshone was gone.

Wally Hughes next vessel was an 80-foot shrimp boat he used for gillnetting swordfish. A big January gale came and caught a lot of boats at sea. I think there were seven boats lost in that storm. In the last message heard from Wally he said one of the big double booms used for shrimping had ripped out of the bow and was swinging wildly. He was going to attempt to cut it loose with a torch. All that was ever found of his boat was a few pieces of floating debris. His luck had run out.

Fishery Politics

I have been involved with fish politics for over 20 years. It is a big can of worms, to say the least, and it is getting worse all the time. More regulations, closures and restrictions are being added every year to reduce commercial fishing. Fewer and fewer boats are working and the fleet is about a quarter of what it was. Except for a few part-timers, no young people are entering commercial fisheries. The part-timers often use rod and reel to concentrate on species that don't require expensive gear and are easy to catch. Their real living is made at other occupations. They sometimes flood the market so the prices drop, Then they return to their shore jobs and the full time fishermen are stuck with low prices.

Environmentalists tried to halt commercial fishing by claiming it was indiscriminate, taking fish of all sizes, large and small. In many instances they were proven wrong. Now they want to "save the ocean" with what they call "complete ecosystem management." This means that not one thing, no matter how abundant, can be taken from a protected area as it could upset the balance of the ecosystem.

The Channel Islands Marine Sanctuary closed areas were recently extended out to six miles. In summer two of these areas outside Santa Cruz are visited by highly migratory swordfish, albacore, tuna, marlin, mako and thrasher sharks, but they cannot be taken there. In the deep bottom canyons and rock piles are rockfish, sable fish, hake and squid that can't be touched. If a swordfisherman sees a finning fish he must check his GPS and if the fish swims into the closed area it is untouchable until it swims out of the prohibited area. If a harpooned fish moves into the closed area the fisherman is forbidden to pursue it. "Educated" people who are "helping save the ocean ecosystem" passed this asinine law. It shows the power of politics and misinformed people when combined.

I was told, "Mike, it is not about fish or people. It is about the federal government grabbing as much of the ocean as it can and saving it to make protectionists happy. Screw the people who lose their livelihoods."

Who knows what will strike on a trolled marlin lure or a baited hook? To me swordfish harpooning is one of the most selective methods of fishing there is. No undersized small fish taken and no by-catch.

Question: When fish are constantly moving, how do you know at any one time what is in a closed area? If there are 100 fish there and three swim out, does that upset the balance? On the other hand, if 100 are there in perfect balance and three more swim in, doesn't that overcrowd the area and upset the balance? The MLPAs moving down the coast will present the same dilemmas. If this pattern continues, I don't have much hope for the future of fishing.

It is all a scam as real commercial fishermen see it, but what do they know about the ocean? They have only spent their whole lives on it and can scan an area and know what is there by observing the conditions: water color and temperature, bait, bird activity, and electronic markings. Many protectionists have never spent time on the ocean, but have read plenty of papers written by people like themselves, so they think they know.

I was doing a dogfish shark survey on my boat with a well-known biologist. He mentioned he was writing a paper on albacore. I said I didn't know he was an authority on albacore. He replied that as a kid he had once caught a few on a party boat, "You don't have to know anything about them. Just read all the papers already written and summarize them," he said. The light bulb popped on!

From the many studies I had read I was aware that they all cited multiple references to other papers. Anyone can write a paper without firsthand knowledge, easy as 1, 2, 3. Read the United Anglers white paper "Ten Bites of the Apple," telling the Fish & Game Dept. how to manage the halibut trawl fishery. Not one person involved with that paper has ever been aboard a halibut trawl boat in California, yet they feel they can tell the F&G, which has been managing halibut since 1907, how it should be done.

United Anglers should look at sportfishing for halibut and the number of fish killed daily by the trap rig and tell the F&G how to manage that. They never will. I wonder why?

What is He Doing?

Each pier, port and harbor along the coast has a fishing community. As time rolls on the communities grow smaller every year. As the older fishermen drop out, no one takes their place. Within each community are different fisheries using different gear and fishermen that are often hostile towards other methods. Even if they dislike each other, they still have a common bond when it comes to opposing activist groups bent on destroying their livelihood. This bond spreads to the adjoining town itself and affects many people other than the fishermen. The supporting customers and supplying businesses depend on the

A pair of fat king salmon that escaped the seals.

Linda and Mike show a nice salmon for sale fresh off the boat.

fishermen for their own prosperity. As fishermen go out of business, so do supporting parts of the community.

My fish buyer introduces well over one million dollars a year into our community from the fish we sell him. Other buyers do the same. The "sport" groups don't care as they have an agenda to rid the ocean of commercial fishermen so they can have it all to themselves.

United Anglers of Southern California recently tried to eliminate halibut fishing by closing our grounds. From 2002 until March 2008, we fishermen worked to show to the Fish & Game Commission our method of trawling was not as destructive as the anti-fishing groups believe. After a long, thorough collaborative study by the Fish & Game observers we proved that our special selective gear and methods did not rape the ocean. The Commission voted three to one to allow us to continue earning a living.

Even though they have no experience or detailed knowledge and discount any evidence contrary to their opinions of how we work, the anti-fishing group was in 100% disagreement on this issue and nothing would change their minds. If they had succeeded nine boats from our harbor would have been out of business and 95% of the halibut catch eliminated for no good reason.

Thankfully, the Commission understands our position and supports us.

The sport group campaigns will no doubt continue until no more commercial fishermen remain in the U.S. Maybe I will be an old man sitting in front of the Maritime Museum mending an old piece o fish netting. People will walk by and wonder, "What is he doing?"

Mike and Linda McCorke, still a fishing family.

141

INDEX

More Books from Monterey Publications

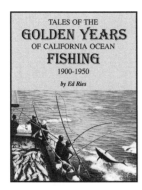

Tales of the Golden Years of California Ocean Fishing 1900-1950 by Ed Ries

Back again after ten years, the award winning second edition of *Tales...* is now available, completely revised, expanded with additional pages, photos, and an index. *Tales...* covers every type of sport and hook-and-line commercial fishing available during the Golden Years. An author with over 200 articles and columns published in *South Coast Sportfishing, California Angler, Mains'l Haul* and others, *Tales...* is the culmination of seven decades of fishing experience and extensive research. This collection is must reading for all who are interested in saltwater fishing and its history. There is no other book like it. *Size: 8.5" x 11", softbound. Pages: 146 with nearly 300 photos and illustrations. $19.95*

ISBN: 978-0-9679247-1-7

Fishing Barges of California 1921-1998 by Ed Ries

Few Southern Californians realize that over 110 fishing barges dotted our coastline from San Diego to Santa Barbara and beyond for three quarters of a century. Vessels that outlived their usefulness were now moored near the coast as platforms from which to fish. The story of each barge, its previous trades under sail and steam, the barge industry, and the fishing of yesteryear are captured in *Fishing Barges of California 1921-1998. Size: 8.5" x 11", softbound. Pages: 104 with over 280 photos and illustrations. $14.95*

ISBN 0-9679247-0-7

Looking Astern by Ed Ries

In *Looking Astern*, Ed Ries combines his lifelong experiences and passion for fishing and 30 years of articles from the column of the same name with photos and stories from friend and fellow fisherman, Mike McCorkle, to make up his third and last book on the fascinating history of sport and commercial fishing in Southern California. *Size: 8.5" x 11", softbound. Pages: 152 with over 300 photos and illustrations. $19.95*

ISBN: 978-0-9679247-2-4

Lost Below; The Southwest's Most Intriguing Shipwrecks, Sunken Aircraft, Submerged Ruins and Undersea Treasures, by David Finnern

Lost Below features the Southwest's most intriguing shipwrecks, sunken aircraft, submerged ruins and undersea treasures. It includes stories about local shipwrecks and various underwater plane wrecks. Steamers and river ports of the Colorado are included, as well as an expedition to the forgotten site of Port Isabel at the mouth of the Colorado River in Mexico. David Finnern is an award winning author with hundreds of articles in *Skin Diver, Immersed, Western and Eastern Treasures, California Diving News, Underwater USA*, and others. He is a former president of the Adventurers' Club of Los Angeles, the California Wreck Divers and a Fellow of the Royal Geographical Society. *Size: 8.5" x 11", softbound. Pages: 104 with over 280 photos and illustrations. $19.95*

ISBN 978-0-9651204-2-5

Order these and other books direct from the publisher: at <u>www.montereypubs.com</u>